WHAT PEC

GOD *of the* IMPOSSIBLE

"*God of the Impossible: The Exceedingly Abundant Life in Spite of Detours!* is an extraordinary book that encompasses the true essence of inspiration and nourishment for the soul. Through the lens of Dr. Marsha Smith's challenges and the thread of her faith, this book takes readers on a transformative journey and faith walk with God. It beautifully illustrates that even in the face of detours and obstacles, there is growth in a relationship with God and awareness that He is providing for us. The author's words resound with authenticity and vulnerability, offering a genuine portrayal of the struggles and the growing relationship with a higher power that sustains and uplifts. Reading this book is like embarking on a pilgrimage of hope, witnessing the remarkable power of faith and being reminded that the impossible can be made possible. It is a profound testament to the resilience of the human spirit and an invigorating reminder that with faith as our guide, we can truly walk through any valley with God at our side."
—Tracey A. Milligan, MD, MS, FAAN, FAES, FANA
Professor and Chair of Neurology, New York Medical College
Director of Neurology, Westchester Medical Center Health Network
Program Director, Neurology Residency

"*God of the Impossible: The Exceedingly Abundant Life in Spite of Detours!*" is a *tour de force.* The authoress recounts her story with a poignant authenticity that grips the reader from the start. It resonates on many different levels, connecting especially with physicians, such as myself, who care for patients with the ravaging illness that is lupus. Dr. Smith's honest and raw telling gives us a glimpse of what it means to live with a chronic painful illness often misunderstood by others. And for those of us who struggle with remaining faithful in the face of adversity . . . her story is humbling and truly inspiring."
—Jennifer Odutola, MD, MSc, Rheumatologist

"The pain that you are experiencing won't compare with the joy that's to come! Does life have you feeling depressed and deflated—like God has deserted you? Then this book by Dr. Marsha Smith is a must-read!

She eloquently explains how to get out of the rut you are in, and it's only by God's amazing grace. Get ready for a powerful and inspiring story!"

—Lorraine D'Aguilar-Heholt
"Auntie Lorraine"

"Dr. Smith does a great job sharing her story and allowing the reader to see God's hand in and over her life. As a believer, this book has inspired me to continue in my PUSH—pray until something happens. With the burdens that come in life, it is easy to turn from God instead of to God. Often times, I feel like I'm alone, but I'm not. Dr. Smith unravels the importance of seeking God and also letting the reader know that the impossible is made possible. What I appreciate most is Dr. Smith's story. In spite of all the obstacles, she overcame them and didn't give up. My faith is greater knowing this, and her book is a true testimony of that. As I am an associate minister in my community, this book will become a resource used to help encourage the congregation.

Thank you, Dr. Smith, for this valuable tool that will empower and encourage lives."

—Rev. Nancy George
Associate Minister of Emmanuel Baptist Church, Bronx, NY

"Is there a silver lining around life's hardships and disappointments? Dr. Smith vulnerably describes her seasons of grief and despair as she walks you through the process of miraculous healing. The purpose of it all is found in the character of your Creator!"

—Pastor Brittany Bowman
Solid Rock Church, Cincinnati, OH

"In her book, *God of the Impossible: The Exceedingly Abundant Life in Spite of Detours*, Dr. Marsha Smith shares her personal journey with raw honesty and vulnerability. Her description of unparalleled faith, following in the footsteps of her mother and grandmother, is truly inspirational!"

—Sarah J. Hon, DO, MBA, FAAN
Vice President, Neurosciences
The University of Kansas Health System

"Be inspired, and be in awe! This is an extraordinary journey of faith, love, and hope conquering unfathomable grief. Courageously bearing her soul to heal others, Dr. Marsha Smith is one of God's miracles in the making!"

—Mingming Ning, MD, MMSC
Associate Professor of Neurology, Harvard Medical School
Director, Cardio-Neurology Division
Director, Clinical Proteomics Research Center

"Dr. Marsha Smith encourages us to embrace our passions and strive for greatness because no matter how big or small our goals may be, we can always make them a reality. In the pages of her book, *God of the Impossible,* I believe you will be inspired to dream big and believe God for the impossible—no matter what obstacles life presents you."

–Kimberly Petree
Pastor, Citygate Church, Lebanon, OH

"*God of the Impossible: The Exceedingly Abundant Life in Spite of Detours!* is inspirational with every page turn. I felt as if God were talking to me through Dr. Smith's experiences. It is a source of encouragement as a honeycomb for the soul. The book provides practical guidance on how to face and prepare for life's challenges through victory in Christ. My faith was strengthened when I am reminded that nothing is too difficult for God. He is not silent. Thank you, Dr. Smith, for writing this book!"

—Samuel Kelly, EA, BSc and Janet Kelly, MPH

"It is evident that Dr. Smith's difficult life experiences—which at times led her to anger and depression—somehow drew her closer to God. Through these circumstances, God has kept and held her in the palms of His hands. I am particularly encouraged by the number of Scripture references incorporated in *God of the Impossible.* They attest to her strong faith and dependence on the Lord."

—Michael Bernard, Pastor
Kingston, Jamaica

"Marsha, you did it; you wrote your book! I am excited and overflowing with joy. 'This is the Lord's doing; it is marvellous in our eyes,' Psalm 118:23 (KJV). I know it was far from easy. As a matter of fact, many were the oppositions you faced in writing it, but what a blessing to see how God has used your trials as a powerful testimony so that you and others can see and know—in a very practical way—that we serve the 'God of the Impossible.'

There is something about writing and making a formal record of our experiences and how the Lord took us through hardships. This book tells your story, but I believe it is a story for your entire family to remember how God has been faithful to you and, by extension, to all of us. It will serve as a compass, a guide, a journal, a history book, a strong foundation, and a source of encouragement to us—but even more importantly, to the younger generation in our family and even for the unborn children to come. 'If God helped Auntie Marsha through all of this, He can do it for me.' This is powerful when I think about it.

"As I read the manuscript, Psalm 34:19 (KJV) came to my mind. I know you are very familiar with this verse: 'Many are the afflictions of the righteous: But the LORD delivereth him out of them all.' Although I have intimate knowledge of your journey—the several struggles, pain, sickness, hurt, and very dark times in your life—I was moved to sadness and tears. However, I am glad I did not stay there but experienced the awesome joy and victory as you've yielded, drawn closer to God, and watched Him transform your life into something beautiful. Indeed, 'nothing is wasted.' I was blessed and edified. Thanks for being obedient to the Lord."

—Olive Andrea Bernard
"Auntie Andrea"

MARSHA SMITH, MD, FAAN

The exceedingly abundant life in spite of detours!

GOD
of the
IMPOSSIBLE

KUDU
PUBLISHING

This book is dedicated to the two strongest women I had the pleasure to call Mother and Grandmother.

I have often said that when God took my mother to heaven, He not only took my mother, but He took my best friend, my confidante, and my biggest supporter and cheerleader. My mother was that person who knew the real me and loved me like no one ever has done. She was the one who always believed in me and saw the best in me but was always honest with me and would point out my weaknesses when appropriate. She inspired me to work hard, to have confidence in and love myself, and to believe that it was possible to attain my dreams. She showed me what it means to make sacrifices for others and to not let a job define who I am but to find my worth in Christ Jesus.

My grandmother was the matriarch of our family. She was one of the strongest women I knew. Widowed with five children, two of them under thirteen and another child with Down syndrome, she had no job. My grandmother demonstrated for me an unwavering faith in God that was matched by nothing else I've seen. She had a prayer life so powerful that when she prayed, we all knew it was just a matter of time before God would answer and act on her behalf.

I have grief, and I still miss them terribly—some days more than others—but I am comforted because while I know that they are not here in the body with me, they are truly home. Glory to God!

"So we are always confident because we know that while we are living in the body, we are away from our home with the Lord. We live by faith, and not by sight. We are confident, and we would prefer to leave the body and to be at home with the Lord."

—2 Corinthians 5:6-8 (author paraphrase)

CONTENTS

Foreword by Blake Mason

Dr. Smith's book, *God of the Impossible: The Exceedingly Abundant Life in Spite of Detours!* offers a refreshing and empowering perspective on overcoming life's detours through faith and a deep understanding of God's purpose. With an insightful blend of personal anecdotes, Biblical references, and practical advice, Dr. Smith invites readers on a transformative journey that inspires hope and encourages unwavering belief in the impossible.

The highlights of this book are Dr. Smith's authenticity and vulnerability in sharing her own life detours and the struggles she faced. Her personal stories create a genuine connection with readers, making it easier to relate to the challenges they might encounter along their own journeys. By intertwining her experiences with biblical teachings, Dr. Smith effectively communicates that detours are not dead ends but opportunities for growth and divine intervention.

The book's central theme revolves around the concept of God's sovereignty and His ability to turn seemingly impossible situations into remarkable triumphs. Dr. Smith skillfully presents this idea with a combination of theological insights and practical wisdom. By emphasizing the importance of faith, trust, and perseverance, she urges readers to embrace their detours and view them as stepping stones toward a life of abundance and purpose.

Moreover, the book is structured in a way that keeps readers engaged and motivated throughout. Each chapter is thoughtfully organized, with clear headings and subheadings that guide the reader through various aspects of the detour experience. This organization allows for easy navigation and enables readers to revisit specific topics of interest as needed.

Dr. Smith's writing style is approachable and conversational, which makes the complex concepts and spiritual teachings accessible to readers of all backgrounds. She avoids excessive theological jargon and instead focuses on practical application, ensuring that her message resonates with a wide audience.

Blake Mason
Worship Pastor, Citygate Church, Lebanon, OH

Foreword by Eric Petree

In a culture that values strength, possessions, and maturity, the greatness of heaven is practically an inversion of what we have been taught to pursue and prize, which leads to some critical questions: What is greatness? Can anyone achieve it? Zig Ziglar said, "You were designed for accomplishment, engineered for success, and endowed with the seeds of greatness."[1] In other words, everyone has the seeds of greatness within them, but those seeds must be nourished and cultivated for greatness to spring forth.

When you think about greatness and limitless living, it's hard to overlook Dr. Marsha Smith. She has made a profound impact on every life she has come into contact with, even my own. Uniquely gifted as a leader who goes beyond the boundaries of the ordinary with kindness, a zeal for excellence, and love for all people.

If you choose to live a life within the boundaries of man, you learn to survive. When things are good, your head stays above water. When things go south because you have been living without margin, you follow suit. Before you know it, you aren't even living a life of restriction; you are living within a deficit.

I've been there. I have wrestled with loss, hurt, rejection, anxiety, and fear. There have been moments that I have doubted the feet God has given me could traverse this thing called life,

---

1 Zig Ziglar, "You," *Ziglar Inc*, 28 Mar. 2017, https://www.ziglar.com/quotes/you/.

much less the road on which I'm traveling. However, over the years, I have prayerfully and intentionally attempted to live a life that reflects Ephesians 3:20. I have tried, not without failure along the way, to trust that my circumstances do not impact my limitless Father's ability to do the impossible in my life. In the pages of this book, you will find that it is Dr. Smith's hope that you do the same.

As you open up and read *God of the Impossible*, open your heart as well. May you be filled with the same hope and determination as Dr. Marsha Smith—that anything is possible!

Eric Petree
Pastor, Citygate Church, Lebanon, Ohio

"Humble yourselves, therefore, under the mighty hand of
God so that at the proper time he may exalt you, casting
all your anxieties on him, because he cares for you."
—1 Peter 5:6-7 (NIV)

Acknowledgments

To my aunt Andrea—You are one of the leading forces behind my writing this book. I am more grateful than you'll ever know. You were the first person the Lord used to plant the seed that birthed the desire I had to write it. You said to me once, twice, and then more times than I can count, "You should write a book, Marsh." Your love and support is a gift and you are a role model in so many ways, but the main one is in your spiritual walk and how you make your relationship with God a priority.

To my aunts Carol and Lorraine—How blessed I am to call you family but more so to call you friends! I am thankful and emboldened each day by our talks and texts, and I pray that you both continue to put God first in all you do.

To the rest of my immediate family—Thank you for your support, encouragement, and prayers! I am grateful for your love and your presence in my life.

To my pastor Eric Petree—It has been a great honor to sit under your preaching, to learn, and to grow in my faith walk with God. The anointing of the Holy Spirit on your life is evident. It is something to be admired and envied. One might ask, "Why?" To use your favorite three words: "The Big Idea." If it is at the top, it will flow down, and if it is in the house, it will be for all the members of the house. Thank you for writing the foreword for this book; I am forever grateful.

To Pastor Kim Petree—Thank you for your words of encouragement and for being a role model of faithfulness and service to God.

To Hannah Zello and Megan Adelson, my writing coaches—I could not have done this without your help and tireless expertise.

To the entire Four Rivers Media team—Thank you for your work on this project. It has been an honor to publish my work with you.

To you, the reader—Thank you for reading this. I pray you, like me, will be inspired to run your race alongside our faithful companion, the Holy Spirit, knowing that we will get a crown!

Lastly, but not in importance, to my Father, God, my Savior and friend, Jesus Christ, and my guide, the Holy Spirit—Thank You! Throughout this project—from its inception to completion—I have asked You, Holy Spirit, to be present in every thought so that Your wisdom would be intricately woven into every letter. I am thankful that You showed up for me, and because of that, I pray that You will be revealed to every reader and that You will transform their lives. Thank You—all three of You—for choosing me. Thank You for loving me. Thank You for dying for me. Thank You for being a constant companion, guide, and intercessor! You are the lover of my soul. Thank You for always blowing our minds and for doing the IMPOSSIBLE!

Introduction

I embarked on the journey of writing this book in January 2021, but in actuality, it wasn't until the fall of 2022 that I began in earnest. I went home to Jamaica, West Indies, in December 2020, as soon as I could after the COVID-19 pandemic started. My aunt Andrea had been encouraging me for some time to write a book, but my nerves always got in the way.

However, on my visit home for Christmas in 2020, she took it a bit further. She gave me a journal in which she had written the message that became one of the biggest pushes for the book. On January 2, 2021, she wrote on the first two pages of the journal: "Your life journey that I have watched over these years as you blossom into your purpose, has been a personal blessing to me. I strongly believe that your life is a powerful testimony that you need to share with others to encourage them. Also, write to record and remember the goodness and faithfulness of our God. More importantly, write to the glory of God."

She then quoted an unknown author, "God has a purpose for your pain, a reason for your struggle, and a reward for your faithfulness. Trust Him, and don't give up." I felt so inspired that when I came back to Ohio, I felt the urge to write. I began my first steps to becoming an author. Unfortunately, all I wrote in the journal was four pages—a rough timeline of my life.

In the summer of 2022, my pastor Eric Petree began a sermon series titled *Are We There Yet?* In it, he spoke about "Destiny: the What," which is a person's purpose fulfilled. Along the road to destiny, he told us that we are first born with "Purpose: the Why." Then, we have to make the right "Alignments" which will affect our "Assignment." Finally, we reach our destiny.

On July 24, 2022, the message that Sunday was titled "Cut the Bologna!" He began the message that Sunday by stating that the message would change our lives. He advised that if we received it and kept our spirits and hearts open, it would change us. It did me! No more excuses! Cut the bologna! Write the book! Therefore, after that series and especially that message, the Holy Spirit's conviction was so strong that I had to—once and for all—be obedient. I knew it was not just a dream my aunt had for me or a dream I had for myself. It was an *assignment*.

If you are like me, you probably have been looked at as a strong person, not needing or wanting anything. Then, hardships happen, and we are left feeling completely overwhelmed, living in survival mode, and barely hanging on. If you have not been considered a strong person, you can still relate to this book because you will have had hardships that led to moments of indescribable pain, heartache beyond words, and depression that threatened to cripple and even kill you if not for hope in the God of the impossible.

I want this book to show you, me, and, ultimately, everyone that it is in our weakness, neediness, humility, and obedience that the Lord can show up and work on our behalf. We probably have asked that a sickness, a death, a divorce, so much more be taken away from us. Probably, we have asked more than three times.

Maybe we—like Paul—have heard the Lord say the following: "My grace is sufficient for you, for my power is perfected in weakness" (2 Corinthians 12:9, CSB).

And we've replied:

Therefore, I will most gladly boast all the more about my weaknesses, so that Christ's power may reside in me. So, I take pleasure in weaknesses, insults, hardships, persecutions, and in difficulties, for the sake of Christ. For when I am weak, then I am strong.
—1 Corinthians 12:10 (CSB)

So, as I've written, I can literally trace God's hand of faithfulness over every hilltop but also in every valley. I hope that, as the reader, you will be able to do the same.

We serve a God of impossibilities, but we will never know that He is a God of the impossible if we never go through wilderness experiences that allow God to show up and show off. God has a track record of doing the impossible. It's on display in the Old Testament with Abraham and Sarah becoming parents in their old age when in the natural, it would have been impossible and with the prophet Elijah calling down fire from heaven to consume a sacrifice drenched in water on Mount Sinai. In the New Testament, we see Lazarus being raised from the dead and Jairus's daughter coming back to life. In these scenarios, if there wasn't death, then we wouldn't have seen the power of God in their resurrection.

Finally, we see Jesus Christ dying on the cross and then, on the third day, arising with all power, having once and for all become the ultimate sacrificial lamb leading to our salvation. If we didn't have Calvary, we wouldn't have salvation and hope for eternal life with Christ.

Have you felt at times, as you are going through trials, that God was silent, or He didn't care? Have you felt that God could have prevented something from happening, but He didn't? Did God answer a prayer with the opposite of what you had prayed for? Can we really get through hardships? Do all things truly work together for the good of "those who love God and have been called according to his purpose," as Romans 8:28 says they do? Has it ever felt like God has abandoned you?

|||||||||||||||||||||||||||||||||||||||||||||||||||||||||||||||||||||||||||||||||||||||||||||||||||

GOD'S SILENCE SHOULD NEVER BE MISTAKEN FOR ABSENCE.

|||||||||||||||||||||||||||||||||||||||||||||||||||||||||||||||||||||||||||||||||||||||||||||||||||

In this book, I want you to discover that the answer to all those questions is a resounding: GOD HAS NOT ABANDONED YOU! In fact, the God of the impossible is closer to us during our times of greatest need, He will provide hope, and He is able to redeem us through the trial. I pray that you will see how, in my own story, God was able to work in my pain and suffering for His glory and my good. God's silence should never be mistaken for absence. I pray that it will encourage you to not give up as you, too, realize that no matter how dark or silent it may seem, God is, in fact, speaking loudly, and as we open our hearts fully to Him by trusting Him in and through the storm, we will be able to see the evidence of His unspoken voice.

In Matthew 19, we find Jesus talking about divorce, blessing children, and speaking to the rich young ruler and then, later, to His disciples. Jesus was having a discussion with His disciples after the rich young ruler went away, grieving instead of deciding to follow Jesus. Jesus was discussing how hard it could be for a rich person to enter the kingdom of God, and that is when He made a life-changing statement: "With man this is impossible, but with God all things are possible" (verse 26, BSB).

I want my readers to always know that nothing is impossible for our God. He is the Romans 8:28 God I mentioned earlier. We will get to realize that throughout our struggles—when we seem to be at our lowest point, we can't get a break, and we begin to think that nothing will turn in our favor. I hope you come to realize that once we surrender all to Him—our dreams and our desires, our pain and our losses, and our health and our very lives—He will do SOMETHING because He is not a God who will just sit and do NOTHING.

My prayer is that we will allow Him to get in our messes, give Him access to all our stuff, and invite Him to take His rightful place on the throne of our lives, being our Lord. We are never abandoned, and we are never removed from God unless we remove ourselves. If God chooses to answer our prayers with a *no* or a *not yet*, then we can rest in His promise that if our lives are truly in His hands, what He has coming and when He chooses to send it will be much more than we could ever ask or think. (See Ephesians 3:20.)

We will realize that during the wait, illness, grief, hardship, or trial, we were building our faith, growing in our intimacy with Christ, resting, and practicing Matthew 11:28-30. I want you to see that it will get easier because as we build our faith and our intimacy with God, we will be primed and ready the next time to turn to God without delay. It becomes easier to trust God with our trials and periods of waiting and silence. I pray that we will learn and never forget the lesson of the eagles, that as we trust in the Lord, we will have renewed strength, and we will SOAR! (See Isaiah 40:31.)

God, our Father, may have put us in isolation so that we can be prepared for the next challenge that will grow us. He could have also been protecting us from unseen danger, and we will be able to look back and see that God was also providing for us the entire time. Even when we didn't feel Him, when we thought He wasn't answering our prayers, He was and will forever be our *Jehovah-Jireh*. Psalm 61, a favorite for many, reminds us that during periods of hardships when we may feel overwhelmed, we can cry out to God and He will hear:

Hear my cry, O God; Attend unto my prayer. From the end of the earth will I call unto thee, when my heart is overwhelmed: Lead me to the rock that is higher than I. For thou hast been a refuge for me, A strong tower from the enemy. —verses 1-3 (ASV)

As we read these words, I pray they will bring comfort now and always, especially during seemingly impossible situations. Always remember the character and promises of God. So often, at Emmanuel Baptist Church in the Bronx, New York, the pastor or worship leader would say, "God is good all the time!" And the church would respond, "All the time, God is good!" I'd like to add another response because I like to personalize things; it helps me in hardships. I'd add, "He's so good to me!" It's a great reminder that we are never abandoned. He will forever be our rock and our strong tower.

As we suffer, well, I pray that this book will also help us to understand that in our obedience, we will come to realize that the lesson wasn't just for us. God will use our hardship to encourage others. Interestingly, before Jesus told us that nothing is impossible with God, He told us, "Truly I tell you, if you have faith as small as a mustard seed, you can say to this mountain, 'Move from here to there,' and it will move. *Nothing will be impossible for you*" (Matthew 17:20, NIV emphasis added). He was telling us that we, too, can do impossible things, but first, we need to have the faith to do them. My hope is that you will realize that with each hurdle and hardship, your mustard *seed* of faith, over time, will grow into a 20- or 30-foot mustard *tree* of faith, overflowing with all the fruit of the Spirit. We will be rewarded with a greater intimacy with God. Why? Simply because we were able to endure, and we suffered well.

As we go through the race of life and encounter hurdles, let's pause and ask God what His plan is. What are we to learn from this? What is it that He is trying to teach us? How will God get the glory from this situation? How is the process refining us so that we can be more like Christ, so that "we all, with unveiled face, beholding the glory of the Lord, are being changed into His likeness, from one degree of glory to another; for this comes from the Lord who is the Spirit" (2 Corinthians 3:18, author paraphrase).

I recently read an article that sums up in a great way how profound it is that we can be more like Christ. John R. W. Stott, in his article titled "The Model: Becoming More like Christ," sums it this way:

There is God's eternal purpose, we have been predestined; there is God's historical purpose, we are being changed, transformed by the Holy Spirit; and there is God's final or eschatological purpose, we will be like Him, for we shall see Him as He is. All three, the eternal, the historical and the eschatological, combine toward the same end of Christlikeness. This, I suggest, is the purpose of God for the people of God. That is the biblical basis for becoming like Christ: it is the purpose of God for the people of God.[1]

So, my friends, I pray that you and I will allow God to do His perfect work in our lives—detours and all. Our faithful Father, our God of the impossible, and the Divine Author wrote in Habakkuk 2:3 (CSB): "For the vision is yet for the appointed time; it testifies about the end and will not lie. *Though it delays, wait for it, since it will certainly come and not be late*" (emphasis added).

||||||||||||||||||||||||||||||||||||||||||||||||||||||||||||||||||||||||||||||||||||||||||||||

SO, MY FRIENDS, I PRAY THAT YOU AND I WILL ALLOW GOD TO DO HIS PERFECT WORK IN OUR LIVES—DETOURS AND ALL.

||||||||||||||||||||||||||||||||||||||||||||||||||||||||||||||||||||||||||||||||||||||||||||||

---

1   John R. W. Stott, "The Model: Becoming More like Christ," *C.S. Lewis Institute*, 30 June 2022, https://www.cslewisinstitute.org/resources/the-model-becoming-more-like-christ/.

CHAPTER 1

The Battle in the Wilderness

"For thou hast possessed my reins: thou hast covered me in my mother's womb. I will praise thee; for I am fearfully and wonderfully made: marvelous are thy works; and that my soul knoweth right well."
—Psalm 139:13-14 (KJV)

"**D**r. Smith, have you seen your scans?" and without waiting for me to reply, he continued, "Well, you would have died if you hadn't come in today." Those were the words I heard as I lay in the intensive care unit bed at Northside Hospital in Atlanta, Georgia, in 2004. The general surgeon's introduction to me is something I will always remember because it is a reminder of how close I came to dying and how God had made a way to preserve my life.

Surprisingly, the first thing I can recall thinking is *How does he know that I am a doctor?* The second thought was, *I am going to die, and I am here by myself.* I believe an inherent fear I had, and I would say most of us have, is the fear of dying alone without our loved ones around us. The second thought stayed with me as more doctors and nurses came into the room, and it really started to sink in how serious this situation was. He hadn't just flippantly stated those words.

It was organized chaos at its best to ensure that I did not die that night. The nurses put in IVs, hooking up antibiotics that were being ordered by the next set of doctors I met. They were infectious disease doctors. The first doctor later told me that I would need emergency surgery because I had ruptured my colon, and my abdomen was filled with infectious material that could and would poison my entire body if it wasn't immediately removed. It seemed like it had been going on for a few days because my body had also walled off a collection of some of this infectious material and formed an abscess.

In less than an hour, I was wheeled out of the room to the operating room (OR). I remember a few friends there as I was rolled out and not knowing how they got there. A urologist whom

I had just met that year was praying for me. In fact, it was his wife I had called that morning to take me to the gynecologist because I was in so much pain that I couldn't drive myself. I had met this couple not long before at a new church that I had started going to in Atlanta.

I had moved to Atlanta in the summer of 2003, and the emergency surgery was happening at the end of spring/beginning of summer 2004. Looking back, they were critical in saving my life that day, and I wish I had stayed in contact with them, but I didn't. I woke up several hours later in the intensive care unit and realized that I now had a colostomy bag. Due to the degree of infection in my abdomen and pelvis, my large intestine couldn't be put back together right away; it would have been too dangerous for my health.

HOW I GOT HERE

I was born in Kingston, Jamaica, to a single mother. My grandmother had my mother when she was seventeen, my oldest aunt ten years later, and then three other children. One of the children is my only uncle who has Down's syndrome. My mother worked in Kingston as a jewelry store manager until I was nine. I lived with my grandmother and her other children in a rural area, about forty-five minutes from Kingston, called Lawrence Tavern. I lived with my maternal grandmother for as long as I can remember until I was aged sixteen.

The story my mom told was that I started to live with my grandmother after I had an illness. My mother left me with my grandmother instead of babysitters. I would see my mom every weekend and then also at least one day in the middle of the week.

Life in Jamaica, like anywhere else, was exciting some moments and, at other times, difficult. We were poor, but we didn't always know it. Surprisingly, there were others who thought we had money because so many around us were even worse off than we were. I remember clearly my grandmother talking about how her sister's church in Florida helped us after her husband had died, how my grandmother would get things on trust at the local grocery store, and how she had nothing some days, but then God would send someone with money or produce for us.

My grandmother would often quote Psalm 37:25 (ESV), "I have been young, and now am old; yet have I not seen the righteous forsaken, nor his seed begging bread." She was one of the strongest Christian women I ever knew and taught us to have a fear and a reverence for God that would last my entire life. She had a faith in God that never wavered, despite life's many storms.

||||||||||||||||||||||||||||||||||||||||||||||||||||||||||||||||||||||||||||||||||||||||

MY GRANDMOTHER WAS ONE OF THE STRONGEST CHRISTIAN WOMEN I EVER KNEW AND TAUGHT US TO HAVE A FEAR AND A REVERENCE FOR GOD THAT WOULD LAST MY ENTIRE LIFE. SHE HAD A FAITH IN GOD THAT NEVER WAVERED, DESPITE LIFE'S MANY STORMS.

||||||||||||||||||||||||||||||||||||||||||||||||||||||||||||||||||||||||||||||||||||||||

I grew up in a Christian household but didn't surrender my life to Jesus until much later. As a child and a teenager, I had to go to church every Sunday unless I was sick. I also had to go to Sunday school, vacation bible school, Sunday evening church, and some midweek services as well. My grandmother was very active in church, and living in her home meant we all had to go. Demonstrating a strong faith, trust, and dependence on God always, she was a Sunday school and vacation bible school teacher. My grandmother didn't work outside the home, but she always gave her tithes and offerings and instilled in us that we were to always give back to God.

Her husband had died when I was six years old, leaving my grandmother with my two primary school-aged aunts and my uncle who was sixteen years old. My oldest aunt was working and lived with us part of the time with her son, who is four years younger than I am. My mother was the other breadwinner for the family. My grandmother rented a house from the husband of one of her younger sisters.

The house was attached to a rum bar, and that was challenging, especially since I was a young girl. When I started to go to high school in Kingston, I felt ashamed of where I lived and wouldn't let anyone come to our house. The bar was open seven days a week, just opening later on Sundays. We obviously had to walk by the front entrance to get home. The bar, back when I lived in Jamaica, was unlike what one would think of a similar establishment in the United States. We were exposed daily to drunken and lewd behavior from the men who frequented the establishment. The men didn't always stay inside; sometimes, they would be outside. Or they would be so loud inside that you couldn't help but hear the vulgarity. Also, the type of music that was played there daily was not always wholesome. So, even though we were living in a "God-fearing" household, we lived on top of and behind an establishment that glorified sinful behaviors. I often look back over my life and must give God thanks for my grandmother and mother who gave me a strong sense of who I am and to whom I belong. That has helped me to now have an identity that isn't based on where I live or what I do but, instead, on my standing in Christ Jesus.

On the first floor of the house, it was situated so that at the front half of the building was the bar, and in the back on the first floor was our kitchen and dining room and stairs leading to a second floor. Upstairs, across the front, ran a full-length veranda. A total of four rooms and one bathroom took up the back verandah. We had a big yard in the back where we washed clothes, hung them to dry, and played. I enjoyed some of my best times as a child growing up playing in that yard. My grandmother's brother-in-law had acres and acres of land that he had planted for crops, and some were sold at the market. We were not always free to pick and eat what we wanted, but we did anyway. We just didn't tell my grandmother.

My two youngest aunts, being only two and five years older than me, were more like sisters to me than aunts. My oldest aunt's son, who is four years younger than me was more of a brother than a cousin. Life was difficult with its many challenges, but we were overall happy. We had many days with no running water and had to walk to a spring to get some, carrying buckets full and making more than one trip on some days. Also, we spent many days without electricity because the government would randomly have power outages. Use of candles and kerosene lamps came in handy during these power cuts. I look back now and cannot imagine how we were able to do it. It was just our reality at the time. It was all we knew and what we had to do to survive.

The gravity of our poverty was highlighted when I passed my Common Entrance Examination, an exam that I had to take to go from primary school to high school. Jamaica's school system is British-based, so we had basic school and then primary school. During the last year of primary school, when I was about ten, each student took a test that helped to determine which high school they would go to. The determination was in part based on scores and to some degree, also based on a student's home address. I passed my exams for a school in Kingston called Queen's High School. It was about a forty-five-minute drive from home. It was there that I saw young girls dropped off for school in cars, some coming out of a Mercedes Benz or a BMW, and it literally blew my mind.

I was living in a home that didn't have a phone. We had no personal cars, and we had to walk to the police station on Sundays to be able to get a call from my mother who was living and working in New York City. As a child living in Jamaica, I learned from my grandmother how to rely on and trust in God even when life was not ideal. She would constantly remind us that He was loving, merciful, and faithful. She was able to say those words even after her husband died and left her with a disabled son, two younger kids in high school, and no income of her own, and even after her oldest child had to move to the US to make life better for the family.

CLOSING ONE CHAPTER AND OPENING ANOTHER

My mother made the decision to move from Jamaica to the United States after the death of my grandmother's husband (not my grandfather). My mother's story of seeking the American dream is no different from so many other immigrants to the US. She came for a better life for herself and all of us since she was also one of the primary breadwinners for our family. My mother moved in with one of her maternal aunts and her family who lived in the Bronx in 1983. Monthly, she would send money to Jamaica to help with bills. She would also send barrels of food and other items yearly, and, oh, the excitement when the barrels were unpacked and we got to see what was in them!

She worked as a nanny and housekeeper for a Jewish family for over twenty years. It was that family who eventually filed for her to get her green card, and when she got it, she was then able to file for me to come and live in the US. My mother had left Jamaica for a better life in 1983, and I was only nine years old at the time. I spent all my summer and Christmas holidays with my mother in the Bronx. It took approximately seven years for the entire process of my mother moving to the US and then me getting my green card and joining her here.

I immigrated in 1990; it was the summer of my sixteenth birthday. My mother worked for one family for several years, but later, when the monies weren't enough to pay all our bills and support the family in Jamaica, she found another job. She worked seven days a week for several years. My mother made such a tremendous sacrifice, working so hard for all our betterment. I now know that despite all that happened and how much I missed having my mother live with me for seven years, during most of my teenage years, it was all part of God's sovereign plan for our lives. It probably isn't how we would have planned our lives, but as King Solomon rightly said in Proverbs 16:9 (AMP): "A man's heart plans his way . . . but the Lord directs his steps."

Even though I had traveled for years to and from Jamaica and New York, it was a completely different experience when I finally moved to NYC permanently. It was so much to get used to, and I had no choice but to grow up. I feel that I became an adult at that time. Initially, when my mom was away at work in Manhattan and later, Westport, Connecticut, I would stay at my grandaunt's home, but that didn't last long. After just a couple of months, I was on my own in the apartment that my mom had rented when I moved to the US. I started spending most days and nights on my own because my mom had to stay overnight at her job. She would come home maybe once a week and then on a Saturday night until Tuesday morning.

It was a difficult transition for sure, going from a home in Jamaica where I shared a bedroom with two of my aunts and lived in a two-bedroom home with my grandmother and the rest of the family. I now had to learn to take care of myself and certain household chores that my mother just didn't have the time to attend to because she was always working. In some ways, it was as if I became the husband in the relationship. I would be the one helping Mom make sure the bills were paid on time, filling out forms for different things, and staying on top of household responsibilities. It was hard at times, and I didn't always enjoy having all that responsibility. I had to decide to be a daughter that my mother could trust when she wasn't at home, night and day, and one that she could depend on to do what she asked.

My mother made the decision to come to America for a better life as I mentioned earlier, knowing that she would get jobs that she could not have dreamed of in Jamaica. Even though my mother didn't read *Psychology Today*, if she had, she would have agreed with Amy Morin, LCSW, a psychotherapist who aptly stated, "When you know who you are—and you are pleased with the person you've become—you'll experience a sense of peace through life's inevitable ups and downs."[2] It simply means we can believe in our self-worth whether we are neurologists or the housekeeper or the nanny.

She had to start doing a job many of us may think is demeaning or beneath us, taking care of someone else's children and cleaning their house and their messes. It was not an easy job, and my mom and I spoke about this on so many different occasions, but she got up and went and did the work. It was very demanding of her time, energy, and over time, even her health. Over the years, she developed significant arthritis in her hands and knees. Some mornings, she had difficulty opening her fingers. Her knees affected her ability to walk and go up and down steps without pain. But she did her job with such grace and to the best of her ability that she was loved, and I would venture to say that she remains loved by that family.

She had to get another job to help us survive and stay afloat financially. In medical school, I watched my mother work so hard. In part, it was so that I could have the life that she never had, and she worked to ensure that my future was better than the life she had to that point. She made a sacrifice for me, and it is one that

---

2   Amy Morin, "How Do You Measure Your Self-Worth?" *Psychology Today*, 11 July 2017, https://www.psychologytoday.com/us/blog/what-mentally-strong-people-dont-do/201707/how-do-you-measure-your-self-worth.

I will always be grateful for. It was one of the reasons why, when I could take care of my mother, I asked her to leave her job and move in with me. It was my turn to take over the financial responsibility of caring for both of us and helping our extended family.

The apostle Paul tells us in 1 Timothy 5:8 (ESV), "But if anyone does not provide for his relatives, and especially for members of his household, he had denied the faith and is worse than an unbeliever." She had worked long and hard and needed a break to be able to enjoy life. It was an honor to be able to show her that her hard work had truly paid off.

SEASONS OF PREPARATION ARE THE PATHWAY TO YOUR PURPOSE

As we go through life, it is wise to look at each stage, each season, as a stepping stone to the next level and to know that we are being changed into what we were created to be. I graduated from the Queen's School, an all-girls high school in Jamaica, when I was sixteen. However, when I emigrated, my mom decided that I should go back to high school for another year, stating I was too young to be starting college.

It was during my four years of college that I believe I grew the most as a person, and certain life values were solidified. It was also during this time that I gave my heart to Jesus Christ, and I became a Christian. I was baptized at Emmanuel Baptist Church in the Bronx. My pastor was Reverend Dr. Major McGuire, III. I lived at home with my mother and commuted from the Bronx to Manhattan to go to New York University. I majored in biology and started my pre-med courses. I always knew I wanted to become a doctor. It had become a dream of mine when I was living in Lawrence Tavern, Jamaica.

IIIIIIIIIIIIIIIIIIIIIIIIIIIIIIIIIIIIIIIIIIIIIIIIIIIIIIIIIIIIIIIIIIIIIIIIIIIIIIIIIIIIIIIIIIII

WE SHOULD NEVER UNDERESTIMATE THE IMPACT WE ARE HAVING ON OTHERS DAILY.

IIIIIIIIIIIIIIIIIIIIIIIIIIIIIIIIIIIIIIIIIIIIIIIIIIIIIIIIIIIIIIIIIIIIIIIIIIIIIIIIIIIIIIIIIIII

When I was six, I had surgery for an inguinal hernia, and the general surgeon made an indelible mark on my life. Just by being and doing what God had willed and planned for his life, he was a role model for me. We should never underestimate the impact we are having on others daily. Chief Justice Sonia Sotomayor agrees:

A role model in the flesh provides more than inspiration; his or her very existence is confirmation of possibilities one may have every reason to doubt, saying, "Yes, someone like me can do this."[3]

I believe it was this encounter at such a young age and several encounters with doctors as a patient during my life in Jamaica that solidified my decision. Once I moved to the US, every step I took was to ensure that I would get into medical school.

Therefore, when my mother insisted I do one additional year, I attended Harry S. Truman High School in the Bronx. I have two high school diplomas, from 1990 and 1991. I spent my year of American high school applying to colleges and was later accepted to New York University. I decided to be a pre-medicine major at NYU, and after graduating with my Bachelor of Arts degree

---

3   Sonia Sotomayor, *My Beloved World* (New York, NY: Alfred A. Knopf, 2016).

in 1995, I started at Temple Medical School, where I earned my Doctor of Medicine (MD) in 1999.

HARDSHIPS ARE PURPOSE REFINERS, NOT HINDRANCES

It was during the summer of 1996, between the end of my first year and the beginning of my second year of medical school, that I started to get sick and landed in the hospital where we started this story as I inched closer and closer to my death. My condition had worsened, and I started to believe that my dream of becoming a doctor would probably never become a reality. I began to doubt what I thought was God's plan.

My illness started with a rash on both of my elbows. During the summer, I was working in a lab, so at first, I was convinced that the rash was probably an allergic reaction to something there. I tried an over-the-counter cream, but when it didn't work over a period of several days, I made an appointment to see a dermatologist. I saw the dermatologist and was given a prescription for prednisone cream. She told me to come back if it didn't work, and the next step would be a skin biopsy to get a definitive diagnosis. Since the cream didn't work, I followed up and had the skin biopsy.

While I was waiting for the various ointments to work, I started my second year of medical school. I was getting additional symptoms such as prolonged joint aches and swelling and fatigue, and the rash persisted. I had seen an internist during this time who told me the symptoms were because I was in medical school. I just *thought* I had these symptoms. I was not sick; it was all in my head. That year *was* stressful, so I also started to believe that my rash, aches, and everything else I was experiencing in my health were just secondary to stress. She had me doubting myself.

Trying to get relief, I started taking ibuprofen when the joint aches became significant. I wasn't getting much sleep, and I was always fatigued. I couldn't seem to get enough rest, even on days when I had gotten good sleep the night before. As I was trying to stay on top of my studies, it became increasingly difficult as my symptoms began to intensify. This further added to my stress level. It was hard to believe the scriptures that I was reading and praying, like Psalm 34:17 (ESV), "When the righteous cry for help, the Lord hears and delivers them out of all their troubles." I wasn't being delivered. In fact, an answer was not easy to come by. What do we do when it seems that even when we're doing the right things, we are being attacked—God's will is being attacked? The first thing is usually one of the hardest, and that is figuring out if the attack is a spiritual attack from demonic forces or simply the effects of living in a sin-cursed world.

I am not sure how long after the biopsy I was called by the dermatologist to follow up with an appointment. She asked, "You haven't been feeling well, have you?" I told her I hadn't and explained about my joint aches, pains, and fatigue. She gave me the report from the skin biopsy. It showed that my connective tissue was breaking down, and she was concerned that I may have an autoimmune disease like systemic lupus erythematosus (SLE). She referred me to a rheumatologist. These are doctors that treat patients with autoimmune diseases.

The rheumatologist did additional testing, including ordering several laboratory tests after reviewing the notes and results from the dermatologist. I went back for those results and, initially, was told that I had an inflammatory process but not specifically SLE. I was given a prescription for stronger doses of ibuprofen to help with the joint aches and pains. The rash on my elbows at this point had gotten better, and there were no new areas, so no additional cream was needed.

It was not too long after that office visit that I got significantly worse. My muscle aches, pain, and joint swelling, compounded by headaches and increasing fatigue, were severe. My mother was still living in the Bronx, so I called her, and she immediately came to Philadelphia. Once she saw how poorly I was doing, we ended up in the emergency room (ER) at Temple University Hospital. My mom sat in the waiting room as I was called by the triage nurse. The nurse took my vital signs and asked the typical questions about why I was coming into the ER. My vital signs were all abnormal, so I was taken straight from the triage area to a room with an ER physician.

Unbeknownst to me, I had a fever. My heart rate was also too fast, so they had to start treatment right away. My mom was eventually ushered back to the room. Out in the waiting room, she had gotten increasingly worried because I hadn't come back. The doctors discussed getting a spinal tap because of the fever, headache, and myalgias, but I refused. I am not sure if I did that out of fear or if I just knew that it was not needed. In hindsight, it turns out it was not needed; I did not have meningitis.

I spent close to a week in the hospital, and it was just prior to discharge that they gave me the formal diagnosis of SLE and mixed connective tissue disorder. I was sent home with steroids and NSAIDS to treat the inflammation and help with the pain. I remember before I left commenting to the doctor that my cheeks looked red. I was concerned about getting the butterfly rash that is so common in systemic and discoid lupus. Once again, I was not believed but was told it was because I had had a fever all week. I was "not to worry."

After a couple more days of being home, I went back to medical school and to my rigorous schedule and requirements. Within a week or so, I did develop the malar rash quite severely on both of my cheeks. Medications were adjusted, a hat was bought because the sun made it worse, and I suffered for several weeks—maybe months—before it went completely away. Thankfully, after it was resolved, I never had another case.

I gained fifty pounds from the high dose of prednisone that I took to control my symptoms. I had to buy high-SPF sunblock and wear hats—even on days when it wasn't particularly hot—to prevent worsening of the rash when it was present and recurrence. It was during these times that my battle/struggle with severe depression, self-esteem issues, fear, and anxiety about my future began.

I was living in Philadelphia without any family support. My mom was in NYC, and my other closest family, grandmother and aunts, my aunt's son, who was like a brother, and my uncle were all in Jamaica. I remember vividly an older family member telling me that I, who now wore a size 16, looked like a pufferfish. Talk about a blow to my already crumbling self-esteem. My middle aunt was getting married, and I was to be a part of the wedding, but I didn't think that I could do it because I felt ugly. I told her that I no longer wanted to be a part of the wedding due to the weight gain. I also had "moon facies"—a swelling of the face, typically seen with prolonged use of high-dose steroids. She was so gracious and said she didn't care; she wanted me in the wedding, and I decided that I should be in the wedding.

I struggled with trusting God and blaming Him for my ongoing illness. Medical school was already difficult. I thought I was hearing His voice and walking in His will, so why was this happening to me? I had the desire to go to medical school to help people with illnesses, and here I was, struggling with my own. During one of the office visits with the rheumatologist after the hospitalization, the doctor asked, "What's your plan B if medical school doesn't work out?"

She asked me to consider changing my career choice because she didn't think I would be able to make it through medical school. She told me to think about other options that would be less stressful and easier for me long term. I told her that medical school was my "plan A, B, and C." So, my answer was a resounding, "No, I am going to stay and finish medical school." I now know that was "holy boldness," based on what I knew to be God's will for my life. Somehow, I knew that despite this storm, I could not go back. I had to push forward, knowing that I could call on Jesus and that if God got me this far, He would lead me through.

I entered medical school wanting to take care of patients with neurological disorders, and during my anatomy class in the first year, I decided that I wanted to become a neurologist or a neurosurgeon. On other visits, as we discussed my disease and my career, I did tell the rheumatologist about my goal to be a neurosurgeon. She told me that the stressors I would encounter during medical school, while conducting my neurology/neurosurgery residency, and when practicing any form of medicine would be too harmful for my health, and she wouldn't advise my pursuing that goal.

It was a real test of my trust and faith in God and what I truly believe was His purpose for my life that I continued in school and didn't listen to what she had to say to me. I didn't become a neurosurgeon, but I stayed in medical school and became a movement disorder specialist in neurology.

|||||||||||||||||||||||||||||||||||||||||||||||||||||||||||||||||||||||||||||||||||||||||||||||||||||||

IT WAS A REAL TEST OF MY TRUST AND FAITH IN GOD AND WHAT I TRULY BELIEVE WAS HIS PURPOSE FOR MY LIFE THAT I CONTINUED IN SCHOOL AND DIDN'T LISTEN TO WHAT THE DOCTOR HAD TO SAY TO ME ABOUT SWITCHING CAREERS.

|||||||||||||||||||||||||||||||||||||||||||||||||||||||||||||||||||||||||||||||||||||||||||||||||||||||

I was already a Christian when I was diagnosed with SLE and mixed connective tissue disorder, and my faith was being tested more than I could have ever imagined. It felt like a full-on assault, month after month, and then what became year after year. I started to question if God truly loved me. Did He really care? Was I doing His will? Did I do something wrong that caused this to happen to me? Was the assault a demonic spiritual attack or the result of living in a sin-cursed world?

I wasn't living a life fully devoted to Christ and His principles. I was half-in, half-out. To be honest, I now realize that I was Christian in name only—not lifestyle. Due to all the studying, I wasn't regularly attending church because I was spending time in the school library. I was praying but not spending quality time reading God's Word, and there wasn't any intimacy in my relationship with God. I did start praying and reading my Bible more after my diagnosis. I needed something—really Someone—to be my "cornerstone" my "solid rock," like the song we sang often at Rose Hall Wesleyan Holiness Church, "My Hope Is Built on Nothing Less." One of the stanzas states:

When darkness veils his lovely face,
I rest on his unchanging grace,
In every high and stormy gale,
My anchor holds within the veil."

And the refrain:

On Christ the solid Rock I stand:
all other ground is sinking sand;
all other ground is sinking sand.[4]

Several scriptures became my lifeline and continue to hold. More have been added through the years. One of them I read or repeated (I had it memorized.) at this point was Philippians 4:13 (NIV): "I can do all things through Christ who strengthens me." I didn't have a car when I was first diagnosed with SLE, and I remember sitting on the bus on the way to medical school, reciting this scripture because I felt so sick going in that I needed His strength and prayed for it daily.

At the beginning of my illness, I was constantly asking, "Why me?" but I knew that my only help would come from the One whom I was questioning. I had to remind myself that He had promised that only He could do more than I could ever ask

4   Edward Mote, songwriter, "My Hope Is Built on Nothing Less," 1834, public domain.

or think. Ephesians 3:20 was a constant reminder that I could depend on Him to use His power that was living inside of me to accomplish what I could not on my own strength.

At the end of medical school, I was accepted into Harvard's neurology residency program, before which I completed a preliminary medicine year at the Albert Einstein Medical Center in Philadelphia. I also finished a movement disorder fellowship at Emory University Hospital. It would take four years of medical school, one year of preliminary medicine, three years of neurology residency, and one year of fellowship training before I was finished with all my studies and could start working as a fully trained neurologist who sub-specialized in movement disorders.

During training, I had so many SLE flare-ups that they were too numerous to count or mention in this book. As a result, I required higher doses of oral prednisone, and sometimes, I would need to get IV Solu-Medrol for three to five days in a row, depending on how bad the flare-up was at the time. They were mainly arthritic in nature and associated with severe joint pains and difficulty walking and sleeping. Later, I also developed pleuritis that affected my sleep and respiration due to the chest pain that happened with just breathing and being in certain positions. I also was diagnosed with pericarditis which is an inflammation around the heart that also led to worsening chest pain and shortness of breath on a daily basis. It was while completing my movement disorder fellowship in 2004 that I came full circle with my opening story, rupturing my colon and requiring a colostomy bag for three months.

On the days that I would get the IV Solu-Medrol, it would run for about an hour or so, and then I would have to go to classes or to the hospital to start seeing my patients. There is one incident that has remained quite vivid, and it happened during one of my away rotations in medical school. I was away at one of the satellite locations and staying in a house with three or four other medical students, all males. Being the only female, I had a room by myself. I had started to notice that my joint aches were getting worse, along with swelling in my knees and ankles mainly. It was coming up on a holiday weekend, and I wanted to drive back to Philadelphia, but I knew I wasn't strong enough to do it on my own. I decided to ask one of the guys in the house if I could ride down with him, and he agreed.

I lived alone in an apartment in an old apartment complex but had a friend who lived in a different unit on the same floor. Thankfully, we had a working elevator that weekend. I was trying to get ready to go back to the satellite location after the weekend away, packing up so that I would be ready when he got there to pick me up. I wanted to take a shower. I had difficulty taking off my clothing, but then I just could not get in the shower. My joints were so swollen and painful that I could not step in on my own. I had to call and ask my friend to come over and help me. My arms hardly worked, so she also needed to help me comb my hair and get dressed due to the excruciating pain.

Once I was back on the satellite campus, I went to bed. At some point during the night, I tried to get up to go to the bathroom, and I fell. My legs just couldn't and wouldn't hold me up. I stayed on the floor for an uncertain period. Luckily for me, it was close to when we would be getting up to go and make rounds on our patients. My housemates noticed that I wasn't coming out of my room to leave, and one of them knocked on my door. I told them what was happening and that I could hardly move, let alone walk. I believe I had gotten myself back into bed before they got up and checked on me.

On my behalf, someone called the director of the program and told them about my lupus and that I was having a flare. The director recommended a rheumatologist in the area and allowed one of my fellow medical students to take me to that office for an appointment. I am sure he pulled strings because it is almost impossible to get in to see a specialist for a new patient appointment that quickly. She saw me that morning and ordered a course of IV steroids for five days. I would start back on my rotation the next day after getting two doses. I had the first dose that day and was able to take the rest of the day off from rotations.

Each morning for the next four days, I went and got IV steroids before going to see my patients and meeting up with my team. We had individual rounds where we saw patients on our own and then had to do team rounds on all the patients with the attending physician. I could not easily sit, stand, or walk up and down the steps, so I would find out which floor everyone was going to be on, find an elevator, and take it to that floor.

It was, once again, an excruciatingly difficult time and one that made my despair and depression so much worse. The prayers of the righteous do, indeed, "availeth much" (James 5:16, KJV). My grandmother, mother, and family prayed earnestly for me on a daily basis, and that helped to carry me through some of the darkest days of my life. Now, it's hard to believe that was only the beginning.

CHAPTER 2

The Lord Giveth and Taketh Away

*"God is faithful, through whom ye were called into
the fellowship of his Son Jesus Christ our Lord."*
—1 Corinthians 1:9 (ASV)

"**C**all home. Your aunt in Jamaica has been trying to reach you and says you're not picking up your phone." As I walked into the office on Monday, September 10, 2012, this was the message that I got from one of the staff. I answered, "Do you know what it's about? I forgot my phone at home this morning; that's why they can't reach me."

It started like most Monday mornings, except it was also my first day back after a week of vacation. My grandmother and my uncle Mark were visiting my mother and me for the summer months. My mother, at this point, had been living with me for about seven years. We had moved from Georgia to Ohio about eleven months prior. My mother, as always, was at the kitchen door that led to the garage as I drove off, and she waved and wished me a great day. She had already helped me get my stuff into the car as she usually did and asked what I wanted for dinner. I asked her to make chicken soup. My mother made the best version of Jamaican-style chicken soup, and that's what I wanted that day. It would have lots of chicken, noodles, yams, boiled dumplings, and corn.

I went to see patients in the hospital prior to starting my office patients for the day. When I got to the office, I was met with all this chaos. I had realized while I was rounding in the hospital that I had forgotten my cell phone and was planning on calling my mother to ask her to drop it off at work for me. I lived only about ten minutes away. As I walked into the office the nurses and other staff were a bit frantic, each saying that my family in Jamaica was trying to reach out to me and that they had called several times. The office staff had tried to page me—yes, an old-fashion pager—but somehow, that hadn't gone through either.

I thought it odd that my family was calling the office when my mom and grandmother were home. I can't remember at this time if I called my aunt first or if I called my home. I spoke to my aunt, and she said my grandmother called and said there had been an accident, but my aunt wasn't sure what had happened because my grandmother was not coherent. I remember calling home and trying to talk to my grandmother, who was in a state of shock, but I couldn't understand anything she was saying. My neighbor, who was there at the house, took the phone from her and started to tell me the story that would forever change my life.

She told me that my mom was in an accident there at the house in the driveway. Someone had called 911, and they had just left with her to take her to the hospital where I was working. My neighbor proceeded to tell me what she knew. Her husband was out in their yard when he heard a loud noise, followed by my grandmother's loud screaming which he heard from the bottom of my driveway, about one-quarter mile away. He came up the driveway to see what was going on. They saw my mom on the ground, barely conscious, so they called 911. The car, at this point, was nowhere near her body but was just on the brink of going over a ditch that was at the side of the driveway. My grandmother was crying hysterically and couldn't tell them much, but eventually, she was able to tell them that my mom had fallen, and the car had run over her.

I was in shock but hung up and told my office manager to come with me because I needed the support. We were heading to the ER when she first decided to call first. The ER staff told her that they decided to take her to a Level 1 trauma center instead. A helicopter was on its way, so we decided to go to the Helipad because I wanted to see her before they took her to the other hospital. We stood there waiting and waiting, but the ambulance never came, so we called the ER again. They proceeded to tell my manager about a change of plans. They were going to a helipad in town instead of the one at the hospital.

She went and got her car so that we could drive into the town. I needed to see my mother before she was taken via helicopter. As we drove, she took a route that took us by the Greenlawn Cemetery. As we were about to drive by, a red ambulance drove by in the opposite direction, going toward the hospital. Something in me just knew it was my mother. We pulled over and called the hospital. Another "change of plans." I felt ecstatic because my first thought was that if there was a change of plans, then it meant she was doing better and no longer needed a Level 1 trauma center. We turned around, drove to the ER, parked, and ran into the hospital. I had only been at the hospital for a few months, but as I walked into the ER that morning, all eyes were on me. It felt as if everyone were quiet. I didn't have to say what my name was; they told me she was in Room 1.

As I walked toward the room, I heard one of the ER doctors say, "Call it." I really don't know how I was able to stand up after I heard that because I knew what it meant. I was at the open room door. A group of doctors and nurses in the room had been working on her. I remember the doctor who was at the bedside near her head and all the equipment that in that short time they were using to help save her life. I started crying as I am doing now as I write these words.

I was given the opportunity to sit next to her, hold her hands, kiss her face, and say goodbye in Room 1 at Southern Ohio

Medical Center at approximately 11:30 a.m. on September 10, 2012. For the first time, I understood clearly what great tragedy felt like and what it meant to "have the rug yanked out from under my feet." I could relate to having the best gift possible and then having it suddenly taken away—no warning and no way to prepare to handle the loss or go on with life after it had happened.

I asked someone to go to my house and get my grandmother and uncle. I was still sitting next to my mother when my grandmother entered the ER, and I can still hear her scream of utter anguish. I know the entire ER was aware that day of our shock and loss that rivaled anything that we had ever experienced, and they were very good to us in our time of grief.

My grandmother was eighty-four years old at the time, and my mother was her oldest child and her dearest friend, and she witnessed her traumatic death. It was several hours later before my grandmother was able to tell me exactly what happened. My grandmother said they had all gone to Kroger to get food for the soup and to send money via Western Union to Jamaica. My mother was not a great driver, and I had a tricky driveway. She would have to drive up, make a right turn, and turn several more times before she would be able to line up the car perfectly to get into the garage.

My grandmother said my mom drove up and partially parked the car in the first garage. They all got out and took the grocery items out. My uncle and grandmother then went to sit on a swing that I had outside that faced the garages. My mother came back out to fully park the car. She said my mom got in and drove further into the garage but not fully. She got out and walked around to the front to make sure that the right side of the car cleared the wall. As she proceeded to get back around and into the car, my grandmother said the car started to reverse.

My mother tried to get in the car to stop it but at age sixty-seven, had severe arthritis and couldn't run, much less jump into a BMW X3 to stop it from reversing. My grandmother saw her fall before the back and then front tires ran over my mother's abdomen. The car was stopped by a slight barrier that prevented things from falling down the ditch at the side of the driveway.

FROM DARK NIGHTS TO DARKER NIGHTS

As I write, it is September 2022, and I remember as I do each year one of the most painful experiences of my life. It's been ten years since my mother died suddenly as a result of the accident. It is so hard to believe how quickly time has flown by and how long it has been since I was able to see and speak with my mother, best friend, confidante, and greatest cheerleader here on earth. There are days that it feels like it was yesterday, and other days, it seems as if it has been more than a decade since I last saw her.

On the anniversary this year, I spoke with one of my aunts, and she said something that really grounded me and caused my spirit to rejoice. She said, "Marsha, it is bittersweet because I so miss her, but I am thankful to God that you made it." It was such a profound and true statement because for so many months, I had prayed for death because the pain seemed so insurmountable and unbearable.

My grandmother and uncle stayed with me for a couple more weeks after my mother's funeral. My mother's sisters, nephews and nieces, and some other family and friends came to her funeral. I was able to go with my grandmother and uncle to Jamaica, a trip I had planned for my mother to take but was able to get the airlines to change. I took six weeks off from work because I was not ready emotionally to return, and even after I started back, it was difficult. I didn't trust my ability to do my job with excellence because I felt so broken. Initially, when I went back, I was not able to go to the ER. I would wait for the patient to be admitted and at that time, do my consult in the assigned hospital room. Once I was able to go back to the ER, I could not go into Room 1 for several months because the feelings were too fresh and the grief overwhelming.

After I got back home from Jamaica and was by myself, the depression got worse. I spent my days either wishing to die or being upset with God for taking away my mother and best friend, all at the same time. I couldn't understand how a God of the family could have taken my family away. My mother was the closest family I had living in the United States, and she was gone. I didn't pray for several months because I was so blinded by the rage and anger I directed at God. I also felt guilty and responsible for her death. I blamed myself for moving to Portsmouth, Ohio, and buying a house with such a difficult driveway.

‖‖

I DIDN'T PRAY FOR SEVERAL MONTHS BECAUSE I WAS SO BLINDED BY THE RAGE AND ANGER I DIRECTED AT GOD

‖‖

Every day while driving, my mind was flooded with thoughts of death. I thought about how I could kill myself. I thought about crashing my car every time that I got in. I remember planning ways of crashing my car that wouldn't lead to anyone else dying. I wanted to make sure it was done in such a way that there wouldn't be any time for EMS to take life-saving measures. I couldn't think of a way of crashing my car successfully that wouldn't hurt other people, so I stopped thinking about that method of suicide.

I then decided it would involve cutting myself. I knew I could do that successfully because at the time, there was no one else in my home. I wouldn't be missed until the next day when I didn't show up to work. I remember clearly getting a large chopping knife from my kitchen. I took it and laid it by my bedside on the table next to the lamp. I finished getting some other things and then got into bed and picked up the knife. The next thing I remember is waking up; it was morning. I had such a feeling come over me. I wasn't supposed to wake up. Why was I waking up and not dead? God had another plan!

Once again, praise and worship songs became my lifeline. "I Almost Let Go," a song by Kurt Carr, aptly describes my sentiments. Its lyrics chronicle a time when the singer felt bound and weighed down by the cares of this world. He didn't see any way through, and he almost gave up—let go. But God's grace and mercy *wouldn't let him go*, so he held on.[5] I truly believe that God's faithfulness is the reason that I am here today—ten years after the death of my mother. It's because God kept me. He wouldn't let me go. His grace and His mercy kept me, and I held on.

---

5   Kurt Carr and the Kurt Carr Singers, vocalists, "I Almost Let Go," by Kurt Carr, released January 27, 2004, track 2 on *Wow Gospel 2004*, Verity Records.

It was after the foiled attempt at my suicide that I decided to seek psychological counseling. I asked my pastor to recommend a Christian counselor. I told him it was for the grief. Anne was a pastor's wife who was also a licensed counselor, and the Lord used her to save my life. I wish I could say I never had suicidal ideation again, but I would be lying. I went for counseling regularly for about a year and then intermittently for six years. I even had certain triggers that would plunge me into depression again when I thought it was over. It felt as if it were a continually repeating cycle, but I continued to fight through it for my sanity. I also realized that I couldn't isolate myself from God anymore. God had never left, but I had closed off my heart and wasn't listening to the Holy Spirit. Instead, I listened and believed every lie the devil was sending my way.

The Lord kept me and carried me through those dark moments when my faith was tested and I wavered in doubt and unbelief. I felt unworthy and unloved. I felt that my mother didn't fight to stay alive that day. When I saw her in the hospital, she had no blood visible anywhere. Her abdomen was distended and that along with the tire marks on her clothing that the hospital had cut off her body were the only signs that something had happened. As a doctor, I knew before the autopsy that she died of internal bleeding.

I felt like my mother had deserted me. I know she loved me and would have done anything for me as she had proven day after day for thirty-eight years, but still, I was believing the lies of the devil. I wasn't praying, but I know others were praying, especially my grandmother, my aunts, other family members, and friends. Intercessory prayers were being prayed on a daily basis.

My grandmother and I spoke daily, sometime multiple times a day, and she would pray, always concerned about me, but I wasn't honest with her about how bad my depression was because I didn't want to worry her. After all that I had gone through, even after I had gotten better, I was still one of my grandmother's biggest worries. Then, she died.

She called me at least twice a day to check in, and we would talk about my mom or things going on in our lives. During one of our many conversations, she started telling me about changes in her stool. I told her it needed to be checked out, my aunts made sure she got in to see a doctor, and she was subsequently diagnosed with bile duct cancer and given only six months to live.

As the doctors predicted, my grandmother died six months later in her own home as was her wish on October 6, 2014. I was blessed to be able to go home to Jamaica to see my grandmother twice during that time and then for her funeral. Even though my grandmother was older, and her death was not sudden, it was still a major loss for me.

I think most of us think of the story of Job and how he suffered whenever we experience extreme losses. As we are faced with an impossible reality, we realize his isn't just a Biblical story. The Divine Author placed the story of Job in the Bible for several reasons; one is that it is an example for us as to how we ought to react when tragedy strikes. Job's life is noted for several things, but one that stands out to me is how remarkably well he responded when he first heard the news of the deaths of his servants, livestock, and even his children:

> *Then Job stood up, tore his robe, and shaved his head. He fell to the ground and worshiped, saying: "Naked I came from my mother's*

womb, and naked I will leave this life. The Lord gives, and the Lord takes away. Blessed be the name of the Lord. Throughout all this Job did not sin or blame God for anything." —Job 1:20-22 (BSB, emphasis added)

I did not respond like Job when I heard about the death of my grandmother, who was also like a mother to me.

Several things stand out in these verses:

1) Job worshiped right after he knew that the unthinkable had happened. He didn't cry or get angry. We don't read that he got anxious or resentful. Instead, he decided it was the appropriate time to worship God.

2) Job realized where his blessings came from and that the giver of all good things was also the taker of those same blessings. In his statement about the Lord giving and taking, we see that Job was not in denial about what had transpired. He was cognizant of the fact that the Lord had a hand in what had happened to his family. However, instead of harboring resentment, Job trusted the sovereignty and providence of God.

3) Isaiah rightfully wrote God's declaration plainly for us: "For my thoughts are not your thoughts . . . For as heaven is higher than earth, so my ways are higher than your ways, and my thoughts than your thoughts" (Isaiah 55:8-9, CSB).

4) Job "did not sin," despite his grief and loss. We cannot allow our grief to take us into sinful and destructive behaviors. Lisa Harper, in her Bible study Job, states: "How we grieve isn't what gets us into troubles; it's what we grieve that can crack the door open for sin to creep in."[6] And author Philip Yancey, in Where is God When It Hurts? states eloquently:

---

6   Lisa Harper, *Job: A Story of Unlikely Joy* (Nashville, TN: LifeWay Press, 2018).

"Pain is a foolproof producer of guilt, I have learned. We all do things we shouldn't. . . ."[7]

5) Job didn't curse God. Later, in Job 3, after his body was affected with terrible boils, we see that he expressed his doubts. We see him giving into despair, and he even went as far as to curse the day he was born. Lisa Harper goes on to say, "Job cursed the day he was born and expressed confusion, frustration and even anger at God over allowing such tragedies to befall him, but he did not reject God."[8]

6) Job didn't give up. As we wrestle with an all-loving but also all-powerful God, we have to remember, "Even if we're on our spiritual backs, we have to keep arching in faith. And be encouraged, because not only is our faith a gift from God, it's more resilient than Gumby—it will stretch far beyond what you think is your capacity to endure. Anguish doesn't distance us from God, giving up does."[9] Yes, we can get frustrated and angry, but don't give up on God.

I had a thing or two to learn from Job because, once again, I started to spiral. First, I lost my mother. Then, the other person that I felt was in my corner, who I felt truly loved and cared for me was taken from me, and depression was pulling me under. Can't we all say we've felt like C. S. Lewis felt after the death of his wife? In *A Grief Observed*, he so eloquently stated:

Meanwhile, where is God? This is one of the most disquieting symptoms. When you are happy, so happy that you have no sense of needing Him, so happy that you are tempted to feel His claims

7   Philip Yancey, *Where Is God When It Hurts?: Coming to Terms with the Tough Times in Your Life* (New York, NY: Harper Paperbacks, 1996).

8   Lisa Harper, *Job: A Story of Unlikely Joy*.

9   Lisa Harper, *Job: A Story of Unlikely Joy*.

upon you as an interruption, if you remember yourself and turn to Him with gratitude and praise, you will be—or so it feels—welcomed with open arms. But go to Him when your need is desperate, when all other helps is vain, and what do you find? A door slammed in your face, and a sound of bolting and double bolting on the inside. After that, silence. You may as well turn away. The longer you wait the more emphatic the silence will become. There are no lights in the windows. It might be an empty house. Was it ever inhabited? It seemed so once. And that seeming was as strong as this. What can this mean? Why is He so present a commander in our times of prosperity and so very absent a help in time of trouble?[10]

My grandmother's death occurred so close to when my mother died and when I tried to take my own life that it was once again a scary time for me emotionally. I struggled with feeling as if God was silent or just absent when I needed Him most, and it seemed disorienting. It amplified the pain that I was already feeling.

I continued to go to the counselor and did grief counseling at my church. I remember that Whitney Houston died the same year that my mom died. At the time, I felt so heartbroken for her daughter. Their relationship and closeness reminded me of the bond I had with my mom, and I remember saying to my mother, "Wow, how sad! I can't imagine how her daughter must feel." Then, ironically, my mother died later that same year, and I had to go through that grief. Whitney Houston's daughter, Bobbi Kristina, then died in July 2015 as a result of drug intoxication and drowning. Her death was only months after my grandmother died. I remember thinking she was brave and stronger than I

10 C. S. Lewis, *A Grief Observed* (New York, NY: Seabury Press, 1980).

could ever be, and I started to think of myself as a failure because I wasn't able to complete what I had started in 2013.

At the time, I couldn't understand why I was going through all these deaths so close together. I would remember different scriptures like Psalm 84:11 (NIV): "No good thing does he withhold," and "Every good and perfect gift is from above," found in James 1:17 (NIV). "God is love," 1 John 4:8 (NIV) and so many other scriptures about God's love seemed like such an antithesis to what was happening in my life. King David is known to so aptly describe what so many of us struggle to put into words, but we know in our hearts:

> *Your unfailing love, O Lord, is as vast as the heavens; your faithfulness reaches beyond the clouds. Your righteousness is like the mighty mountains, Your justice like the ocean depths. You care for people and animals alike, O Lord. How precious is Your unfailing love, O God! All humanity finds shelter in the shadow of Your wings. —Psalm 36:5-7 (NLT)*

I thought if God really loved me, He would not have taken my grandmother so quickly after my mother. In *Where is God When It Hurts?* Philip Yancey states, "How can a loving God allow this to happen? Either God is all-loving or all-powerful, but he can't be both."[11] And herein lay my struggle. In some ways, I felt betrayed by His double taking, and I questioned, *Why would God withhold my joy, my peace, and why would He take away the two women in my life who loved me more than any other human being ever would?* I recognized that being born to my mother was, indeed, a gift from God. He could have chosen another mother and grandmother for me, but He chose the best ones. Still, I could not—for

---

11 Philip Yancey, *Where is God When It Hurts?*

a long-time—grab hold of the fact that in His sovereignty, He did have the right to "taketh away."

C. S. Lewis wrote:

Praise is the mode of love which always has some element of joy in it. Praise in due order; of Him as the giver, of her as the gift. Don't we in praise somehow enjoy what we praise, however far we are from it? I must do more of this. I have lost the fruition I once had of H [Lewis's wife]. And I am far, far away in the valley of my unlikeness, from the fruition which, if His mercies are infinite, I may sometime have of God. But by praising I can still, in some degree enjoy her and already, in some degree, enjoy Him. Better than nothing."[12]

WHEN THE DEVIL FIGHTS, FIGHT BACK

Breaking the stronghold of depression is like doing an obstacle course, or at times, I like to think of it like fighting a battle. I realized after I took up that knife, determined to end my life, that somehow, I had allowed the pain from the sudden death of my mother to create this stronghold of grief that eventually became a stronghold of depression. I am not saying that every depression is a spiritual stronghold; I know that quite well. As a neurologist, I know that depression is often due to chemical imbalances—not spiritual—requiring medications for treatment. I believe wholeheartedly that God can and will use medications in some cases to bring about healing from depression. However, as a Christian, I was also able to recognize this spiraling as a cry for help, and finally, I found the help that I needed.

---

12 C. S. Lewis, *A Grief Observed.*

||||||||||||||||||||||||||||||||||||||||||||||||||||||||||||||||||||||||||||||||||||||||||||

BREAKING THE STRONGHOLD OF DEPRESSION IS LIKE DOING AN OBSTACLE COURSE, OR AT TIMES, I LIKE TO THINK OF IT LIKE FIGHTING A BATTLE.

||||||||||||||||||||||||||||||||||||||||||||||||||||||||||||||||||||||||||||||||||||||||||||

I asked my pastor at the time because I knew I wanted a counselor who was a Christian, and I also knew that my mental, physical, and spiritual health needed healing. He recommended someone who was in a different city, the wife of a pastor and also a licensed counselor. She became paramount in my healing; she was truly a gift from God. I can see how He orchestrated each visit and used her to show me that my life had meaning and that my mother's death was not the death of me. He would help me through this pit, and I started to have hope that He would continue to bless and preserve my life. I began to see that my life had a purpose and that it was not finished. I was created on purpose for a purpose, and the Lord still had more for me to do. That work happened during those many sessions, spanning over a few years, but also the work I had to do on my own after the sessions were finished.

I began using my alone time as my own counseling sessions instead of having pity parties. I had to lose the victim mindset and get rid of the anger. I had to choose to process the loss, grief, and pain in such a way that I was moving on toward victory. Left to myself, I was giving the devil a front-row seat in each internal conversation, and as you can imagine, it was always doom and gloom. The devil, each and every day, was stealing my joy, and I was allowing it to happen. You read correctly. I wrote "allowing" because that is what we do when we decide to listen and believe the lies of the devil and permit those conversations to dictate our actions. We must realize that we do have the power to make the decisions that will crush the devil and his evil taunts and give us the freedom that we crave.

It was because of those alone times that I chose to spend time with the Holy Spirit, I chose to read the Bible, and I chose to allow God's presence to calm the fear and kill the anger living inside of me. I can see now that the Lord had a plan and purpose for my life, but the devil was fighting it all along. C. S. Lewis did not give up. Instead, he wrote:

> And so, perhaps with God. I have gradually been coming to feel that the door is no longer shut and bolted. Was it my own frantic need that slammed it in my face? The time when there is nothing at all in your soul except a cry for help may be just the time when God can't give it: you are like the drowning man who can't be helped because he clutches and grabs. Perhaps your own reiterated cries deafen you to the voice you hoped to hear.[13]

The devil knows that if he can't get us off course, depressed and doubting God, then it is another nail in his coffin, and he has no idea what will happen next—what greatness God has in store for us, whose life we will impact next—and he is nervous, So he keeps trying to derail us. Marvin Sapp's song "Never Would Have Made It" is so appropriate and true for my life. Like him, I'm stronger,

---

13 C. S. Lewis, *A Grief Observed*.

wiser, and better, and when I look back over all God brought me through, I can see that He was the one I held on to.[14]

WHEN YOU DON'T WANT TO, DO IT ANYWAY!

Jesus Christ told us before He left this earth that He would be sending our Advocate, Helper, Comforter, Intercessor, Counselor, and Strengthener in the form of none other than the Holy Spirit. (See John 16:7.) He also promised that He, the Holy Spirit, would be in close fellowship with us. I love that different translations use different words to describe the Holy Spirit in his verse. The different titles highlight for us so many ways that the Holy Spirit can intervene on our behalf. Have we benefited from the Holy Spirit in the way God intended us to experience His presence living inside of us?

I admit that I wasn't but knew that I had to start doing that so that I could start to break the strongholds in my life. For a period of time when I was in medical school, I only listened to gospel music in my car, but I had stepped away from that. I knew I had to guard my ears—not just from my own words but also from what I allowed myself to watch and listen to. I have to say that even though the songs I listened to weren't songs that had curse words, they were not uplifting or glorifying God, and for me, at that season of my life, I knew that I needed to stop listening to them for my recovery. I had to saturate my spirit with God—with His presence—and it wasn't always easy. I didn't always do a good job, and some days, I flat-out failed.

---

14 Marvin Sapp, vocalist, "Never Would Have Made It," written by Matthew Brownie and Marvin Sapp, released July 12, 2007, track 12 on *Thirsty*, Verity Records.

I didn't conquer everything all at once. It is a process that continues. Even now, I am trying to be mindful of what I watch—and what I read, especially. Each of us must listen to the Holy Spirit and follow His leading as He guides each of us differently in certain areas and during specific seasons, so I am not trying to be legalistic in my viewpoint. I also realize that what I needed at that stage isn't for every season. I'm still mindful of what I am allowing to have influence over my thought life, whether it be intentional or unintentional. God's Spirit was witnessing to my spirit that I could hold on with His strength, power, and guidance. All I needed to do was let go of the reins, relinquish control of my life, and choose to be a living sacrifice, which we are told is true worship. (See Romans 12:1.) In this form of worship, we open the door of communication between God and ourselves. (See Revelation 3:20.) We then get to truly experience the presence and power of God. It allows us to communicate more openly because worship is the means through which we invite God's presence into our lives and into our world.

It was hard to worship through the storm, but I know that it was important back then, and it remains an important tool for me as I go through other hardships in my life. It will be the same for you as well. On days when I would wake up and feel so down and at times when I felt full of guilt about my mother's death, I turned to praise and worship songs, reading scripture, and praying. I might not have felt like doing it all the time, but I would listen and read a devotional that would include scripture.

I can recall so vividly on many Sundays after my mother died that I didn't want to go to church, but I would get up, get dressed, and go. Invariably, it was those Sundays that I would get such a word from God. I would feel His presence the strongest, and I would be the one saying, "I am so glad I went to church." I noticed that once I got started, over time, my mood would elevate, and what initially seemed like I was being fake became something that I enjoyed and looked forward to doing. You might have heard the term, "Fake it 'til you make it," and it may have negative connotations, but for me it didn't because those Christian disciplines of worship and Bible reading allowed me to "make it."

In Romans 4:17, we are to call things that are not as though they were; for me, that included waking up and making decrees over my life. We can all do this, and it is, in essence, speaking scriptures and God's promises over our lives and, when possible, personalizing them so that they have even more meaning for us. Some of the decrees that I have used are as follows:

- » "This is the day that the Lord has made, I will rejoice and be glad in it!"—based on Psalm 118:24
- » "By His stripes, I am healed!"—based on Isaiah 53:5
- » "God, I thank You because You have healed my broken heart."—based on Psalm 147:3

It is so amazing how God works, and I will say—even now—He never ceases to amaze me, and it never grows old!

HE REDEEMS AS YOU TRUST

Another reason I was able to get ahead of and over the major depression was by being able to trust God—even when He didn't seem to be trustworthy, when He didn't seem to be working in my favor, when it felt like He wasn't answering my prayers, and that He didn't care. We have to rely on the God we know that He has been in the past. We trust what we read in the Bible. I had to look beyond the obvious and notice God's blessings in my life despite what I might have chosen to believe that was fueling my depression.

Psalm 5:11-12 (NLT) says,

But let all who take refuge in You rejoice; let them sing joyful praises forever. Spread your protection over them, that all who love Your name be filled with joy. For You bless the godly, O Lord; You surround them with Your shield of love.

Blessings aren't just about abundant finances, perfect health, a happy family, or a blissful marriage. They can take on many different forms. A blessing is being a child of God, knowing that Jesus Christ died for my sins, and I have an eternal home with Him. It is having the Holy Spirit living inside of me, having the love and protection of God as a shield, and waking up each morning, knowing that I am being given another opportunity to make a difference in the world. Being able to think clearly, having the rest of my family, friends, a church family, a job, a car, and a house, and despite having systemic lupus, being able to work and make a difference in the lives of my patients are all blessings.

My mother was dead, and I missed her greatly. I was battling depression, life as I knew it no longer existed, and I had a new normal for my life that did not include her presence, but God was still on His throne, He still had my heart, and He will forever stay there. Therefore, I chose to worship Him and trust Him. I encourage you if you are in the midst of your season of doubt and depression to, first and foremost, choose to TRUST and WOR-SHIP God. Your freedom and maybe even your life depend on it!

My being able to get through that season of depression and suicidal ideation was based on several different things all working together and life situations all orchestrated by God. As we get beyond each storm, we should be able to look back and, like Joseph in Genesis 50:20 (NIV), be able to say: "[The devil] intended to harm me, but God intended it for good to accomplish what is now being done, the saving of many lives."

Something that stood out to me, and that you may have noticed already in that verse, is part of what Joseph said to his siblings. He said that his suffering took place "to accomplish what is now being done." Here it is; part of the crux of our Christian lives is realizing that what we go through is all part of a divine plan; it is not all about us. God will always find a way if we are willing to partner with Him to use our lives to accomplish His will here on earth, and His will always comes to pass. We just have to decide to be a part of it. I have learned many things along this painful way, and I hope that you will also learn some as well.

DEAR YOUNGER ME

Most of us have probably been in a job interview and been asked, "What would you say to your younger self?" I have, in the past, thought, *What a weird question! Why would I want to speak to my younger self? I want to live my life forward, not backward.* However, I have realized it's not so much talking to our younger self but realizing what we have learned so far from our life experiences. They should be words that I would tell my future self. So, here's what I would say to my younger self but really what I want my future self to know:

Hang in there; it's going to get bumpy. It is going to be downright scary at times, but it's going to be the ride of your life. During all the ups and downs, if you don't give up, you will see God work in

*such a miraculous way that you will have no choice but to sit back,
worship Him, and crave His presence! In His presence, there is
fullness of joy, and, yes, at His right hand are treasures that will
never run out, so stay close. Abundant life is yours, and freedom
of mind and standing on God's Word bring abundant life.*

RENEWAL OF THE MIND RETURNS WHAT WAS STOLEN

After all that I had gone through and learned, I was in a much
better place in my relationship with the Lord, compared to when
my mother died suddenly, when the devil attacked again. I was
reading the Bible, praying, and having my quiet time, so this time,
I immediately recognized the lie. We know that the devil "is a liar
and the father of lies because there is no truth in him" (John 8:44,
author paraphrase). I had to learn to recognize truth from the lie.
In order to do that, however, I had to know truth.

Jesus Himself reminded us in His own words, "I am the way,
the TRUTH, and the life" (John 14:6, NLT, emphasis added).
Our life depends on having an intimate relationship with Christ
Jesus who is "The TRUTH." Yes, we know the dictionary's definition of truth, but we also know the One who is "The TRUTH."

God's truth, also in His Word, is what we must saturate our
heart, mind, and emotions with on a daily basis so that we can
rest in His promises and have Him fight our battles. Philippians
4:8 (CSB) is also another practical way to stay in the truth:

*Finally, brothers and sisters, whatever is true, whatever is hon-
orable, whatever is just, whatever is pure, whatever is lovely,
whatever is commendable—if there is any moral excellence and
if there is anything praiseworthy—dwell on these things.*

Other translations may have "meditate" or "think" on these things. This is so practical, right? God knew that the devil would try to inundate our thought lives with his lies and negativity, so right there, He spelled out for us one of the ways that we can win and allow Him to fight for us. He came that we could find rest in Him. (See Matthew 11:28.)

I am reminded of a message that Pastor Eric recently gave. His sermon was based on the scriptures found in Acts 12. He talked about being able to sleep between problems. Peter was imprisoned before a trial that, presumably, would have led to his death, but Peter slept while bound with chains between two guards. Peter, the impetuous disciple, the I-am-going-to-walk-on-water kind of guy, and the I-am-and-will-cut-your-ear-off guy was sleeping while facing death. He, in that moment, is an example of what it looks like to truly believe that we can and will find rest in God. He slept with full assurance that the God he served would fight his battles.

I chose that day to listen to the voice of the Holy Spirit, and I rebuked the devil. I started to believe that my life did matter, God had more for me to do, my family that was still alive loved me, and I wanted to be alive. Once again, I had to look to the Word of God and use it as the sword it is, according to Ephesians 6:17. I started to do as Peter admonished in 1 Peter 5:6-7, casting all my anxieties, fears, and worries on Jesus because I knew He cared for me.

I hadn't been seeing the counselor as much at this time, but when this happened, I reached out to her. I was able to get an appointment that day, attended a series of appointments, and continued with her for several years until I moved. When I saw her and told her at the appointment why I reached out, I remember her saying, "I was thinking about you when I heard [about Bobbi Kristina's death] and wondered if you were going to reach out for an appointment." She understood how that would have triggered emotions in me at that time.

As Christians, we are overcomers because of Calvary, and we no longer have to listen to the lies of the devil. Consider this conversation between Job and his wife:

His wife said to him, "Are you still trying to maintain your integrity? Curse God and die!"

But Job replied, "You talk like a foolish woman. Should we accept only good things from the hand of God and never anything bad?" —Job 2:9-10 (NLT)

You and I are *more than conquerors,* and as we accept adversities from God, we know that we have Christ. Instead of listening to the voice of our adversary, who is only there to "steal and kill and destroy" (John 10:10, NIV), we must take back what he has stolen by renewing our minds and being strengthened with God's promises:

> » We can do all things through Christ. —Philippians 4:13
> » We are loved more than we can comprehend. —Ephesians 3:19
> » We are never alone. —Matthew 28:20
> » He heals the brokenhearted. —Psalm 147:3
> » He cares about the anguish of our soul. —Psalm 31:7
> » He is coming back one day. —John 14:3

One of the most comforting scriptures is found toward the end of the Bible. The Divine Author, as He closes the book of Revelation and His love letter to us, leaves us with a promise that will always bring hope and help us in renewing our mind during times of grief, loss, fear, anxiety, and depression. We can rest in His promise found in Revelation 21:4-5 (HCSB):

> *He will wipe away every tear from their eyes. Death will be no more; grief, crying and pain will be no more, because the previous things have passed away.*
>
> *Then the one seated on the throne said, "Look, I am making everything new." He also said, "Write, because these words are faithful and true." Then he said to me, "It is done! I am the Alpha and the Omega, the beginning and the end."*

YOU ARE BECAUSE HE IS

We live in a fallen world, so pain is inevitable and so are disappointment, death, and failure. How we react varies and can and will affect how we walk through these seasons of life and how we receive it after we have gone through. However, there is a big BUT: I can choose to see the I AM in every situation. Christ Jesus describes himself in seven "I AM" statements that I urge myself and us all to remember. They are all recorded in the book of John:

1) I am the bread of life. (6:35)
2) I am the light of the world. (8:12)
3) I am the door of the sheep. (10:7-9)
4) I am the good shepherd. (10:11 and 14)
5) I am the resurrection and the life. (11:25)
6) I am the way, the truth, and the life. (14:16)
7) I am the true vine. (15:1-5)

In every hardship—*whatever* it may be—I need to remember that God the Father, God the Son, and God the Holy Spirit is the great I AM. In the Exodus encounter, before Moses confronted Pharaoh, he had to first confront the Israelites. He was concerned that they would not believe that God had sent him. Moses's conversation with God went like this:

> *Moses said to God, "Suppose I go to the Israelites and say to them, 'The God of your fathers has sent me to you,' and they ask me, 'What is his name?' Then what shall I tell them?"*
>
> *God said to Moses, "I AM WHO I AM. This is what you are to say to the Israelites: 'I AM has sent me to you.'"*
> —*Exodus 3:13-14 (NIV)*

||||||||||||||||||||||||||||||||||||||||||||||||||||||||||||||||||||||||||||||||||||||||||||||||||||

I CAN CHOOSE TO SEE THE I AM
IN EVERY SITUATION.

||||||||||||||||||||||||||||||||||||||||||||||||||||||||||||||||||||||||||||||||||||||||||||||||||||

I remember as a child thinking, *That makes no sense*, but I thought that *a lot* about certain parts of scripture. As an adult who has gone through some things and as one who has surrendered her life to Christ, it makes a lot of sense. I can look at the story that begins in Exodus 3 and then go back to the book of John and read the red letters of Jesus Christ—the embodiment of I AM WHO I AM. I can be reminded through life's hardships and tribulations that I serve a God who has all power and who—just at the mention of His name—causes demons to shake. (See James 2:19.)

I can walk with Him, who is the bread of life, when life seems without substance. I walk with Him, who is the light of the world and who will illuminate my path, if I just ask for wisdom, guidance, and counsel. He is at the door knocking and waiting to come in and just sit with me. I have an open invitation to come to Him with every need at any time because "the veil of the temple was torn in two from top to bottom" (Matthew 27:51, BSB). He is my good shepherd, and He will always provide and protect me along the road of life.

We have to remind ourselves as Christians that we walk with Him who is the resurrection and the life and who brings life to every dead thing in our lives. We walk with Him who is THE WAY, THE TRUTH, and THE LIFE. When faced with trials and tribulations, I know that I already have One with me who IS truth and who IS life, so I don't have to listen to the lies of the devil. Instead, I can choose to walk in THE WAY, and that way leads to abundant and eternal life.

PREPARATION IN THE FORM OF QUESTIONS

For many days, I thought God didn't care enough to stop what had happened. I wondered, *Why did He not prevent my mother's death? Why did she have to die in such a horrible way? Why did I not die with her? Why leave me to suffer and be alone? Why take my grandmother so quickly after my mother's death?*

Many of my questions weren't even logical. I thought about how my mother didn't fight to stay alive—to stay with me— so that meant she didn't really love me. I thought about her in heaven, no tears and no pain, and me on earth praying for death because of my incessant grief. It meant that I really wasn't as loved as I thought I had been by my family or by God if He allowed this to happen.

I carried the guilt of moving to Portsmouth until the Lord healed it all. I can say, like Paul in Philippians 1:6 (AMP) that "I am convinced and confident of this very thing, that He who has begun a good work in you will [continue to] perfect and complete it until the day of Christ Jesus [the time of His return]. God's faithfulness never failed, He stood by every promise, and He has continued to be my sole source of survival. In John 16:33 (NKJV), Jesus promised that "these things I have spoken to you, that in Me you may have peace. In the world you will have tribulation; but be of good cheer, I have overcome the world."

In life, we can expect storms and challenges, but I have realized that it is best to prepare for the challenges or tests before they come. It took me several years before I was able to start practicing as a neurologist. I had several tests along the way that prepared me to be successful as a physician. I continue to attend conferences and take continuing medical education courses to stay up-to-date on the changes in medicine. It is also a way that the US allows me to keep my licenses to practice medicine.

I find it to be the same in our spiritual lives. We know that James said in James 1:12 (NIV), "Consider it pure joy, my brothers and sisters, whenever you face trials of many kinds." How can we be joyful during trials? I believe one way is that we can be ready before they come. We have to keep our hearts and minds on things above, spending time in worship with songs and in constant communion, praying, and reading the Bible. I have found that I have to be able to recite Bible verses at random times, and they become vital to sustaining a healthy mind. Hold on to the anchor that will hold through every test and trial.

I have gone through several periods of time when I decided to only listen to gospel music in my car. I still primarily do that in an effort to keep my mind, will, and emotions in a healthy place spiritually. That will lead to a healthier life physically also. I am not saying everyone must do that, but for me, and in those seasons of my life, that was one way that I found helped me to keep my mind stayed on Him. It was how I was able to keep God's peace, love, and faithfulness foremost in my thought life.

Laura Story's song "Blessings" was a lifeline. I listened to it often and was able to see her live, and what a blessing it was to hear her testimony that led to that song. If we stop and meditate on our tribulations, we can also say that it's possible God's blessings come through raindrops, tears, and sleepless nights because, without them, we would never feel God's closeness. If I had considered every tribulation a "mercy in disguise," I may have faced every hardship differently.[15] I wouldn't have spent years asking, *Why me, Lord? Why am I the one facing SLE diagnosis, constantly in pain and having to take medications? Lord, what did I do wrong that I have to suffer through these things? Lord, I feel as if you are constantly throwing things at me that I can hardly bear?* and so many more questions. The most resounding one was, *God, where are you? Are you listening to me?*

The questions ultimately left me feeling sorry for myself and even putting blocks between my Heavenly Father and me. If I was able to prepare for the trials by spending quality time in God's Word, then, when trials come, one of my responses would be, *God, what are you trying to teach me during this?* I would spend

---

15 Laura Story, vocalist, "Blessings," by Laura Story, released February 21, 2011, track 5 on *Blessings*, INO Records.

more time in His presence, in worship and in gratitude because I would know beyond any doubt that He would use it for His glory, and, ultimately, it would also be for my good. I would spend more time reciting the promises found in His Word. I would be reminded that the Lord is near to those who have a broken heart (Psalm 34:18). I would be reminded that He comforts those who are afflicted (2 Corinthians 1:4). We would be encouraged to not give up, "even though my outer person is being destroyed because my inner person is being renewed daily. Momentary light afflictions are producing an absolutely incomparable eternal weight of glory (2 Corinthians 4:16-18, author paraphrase).

In order to allow us to have the abundant life during trials and tribulations, I have come to learn (and it is not easy) to reframe each situation in light of God's mercies and promises. I have to remind myself that He promised that He would never leave me nor forsake me. He is "not a man that He should lie," and I know that if He cannot lie, then every promise in His word is true. "Or has He spoken, and will He not make it good?" (Numbers 23:19, NKJV).

BE STILL, AND KNOW THAT HE IS GOD

While we all have different times of the day that we feel are better than other times to sit and be quiet with the Lord, it is very important to be thankful to and to check in with God before we start the day. It allows us to set the tone for the day. It reminds us that we can do nothing without God that will be meaningful without His Holy Spirit guiding us through it all. Jesus knew how much we would need the Holy Spirit, so He made sure that we would never be alone prior to His Ascension. In John

14:16-17, Jesus speaks about the coming of the Holy Spirit. He will be our advocate and with us forever if we love Him and keep His commandments.

If we are spending time in daily communion with the Holy Spirit, we are then made aware of God's thoughts. He can teach us, guide us, and also pray for us when we don't have the words. Holy Spirit illuminates the meaning of God's Word so that I can come alive during my daily walk.

||||||||||||||||||||||||||||||||||||||||||||||||||||||||||||||||||||||||||||||||||||||||||

IF WE ARE SPENDING TIME IN DAILY COMMUNION WITH THE HOLY SPIRIT, WE ARE THEN MADE AWARE OF GOD'S THOUGHTS.

||||||||||||||||||||||||||||||||||||||||||||||||||||||||||||||||||||||||||||||||||||||||||

In the rearview mirror, we will be able to say, like the song, "Your grace and mercy brought me through, I am living this moment because of You."[16]

---

16 The Mississippi Mass Choir, vocalists, "Your Grace and Mercy Brought Me Through," by Franklin D. Williams, released October 20, 2005, Malaco Records.

CHAPTER 3

Discerning God's Voice in the Detours

*"The Lord your God is in your midst, A victorious warrior.
He will exult over you with joy, He will be quiet in His
love, He will rejoice over you with shouts of joy."*
—Zephaniah 3:17 (NASB)

How do we get better at discerning God's voice? All too often, the fear of making wrong decisions because we missed God's voice becomes paramount to us as believers. We all want to be good at discerning God's voice among all the other voices that we are bombarded with on a daily basis. Being able to discern God's voice will help us as we make life decisions: Which college should we go to? Should we marry this person? Which job should I take? What career path should I choose? And the list can be quite exhaustive. I would worry that if I did miss God's voice, my life would be forever ruined, and there would be no way of correcting it. I constantly lived with the fear of missing God's voice. I would look at trials and hardships as dead ends instead of thinking of them as detours.

Detours can show up looking like illness, death, or hardship of any sort that we know we will have in our lives. (See John 16:33.)

DO NOT DOUBT YOUR GPS

If we look up the definition of detour as it pertains to driving directions, it typically means that the navigation device we are using will consider the current traffic conditions to give us the shortest time to our destination. In discerning God's voice, especially during hardships, we must pay special attention so that we don't ignore or mislabel God's detours and keep going the way we want to go. We must heed His directives so that we get to our purpose—even if it is by a more circuitous route—because if we decide to go on our own, it may take us a much longer time and with more unnecessary hurdles.

Detours may seem like a long, arduous, totally unnecessary route to get us to where we need to go. Going back to our analogy of driving, if we see a sign that says "Detour," it always means that if we continue going in the same direction, we are either going to get to a point where we can't go any further, or we may end up going over a cliff or hitting high-level water. We either end up dying, or the journey becomes longer because we encounter obstacles that we could have avoided or that we were warned about.

We may choose to ignore the detour signs because we are concerned that detouring would take too long, or the route is too long. We assume that we know more than the Department of Transportation, and it really can't be as bad as they are suggesting it will be if I just continue on the path that I have already planned. Now, in my car and in most cars nowadays, we have a global positioning system (GPS). If it's not part of our cars, then it is probably an app on our phones. I rely more on my GPS when I am going someplace new or when I unexpectedly meet up with an accident or construction. My GPS can give me turn-by-turn directions. These apps also have the capability to reroute us if they sense that up ahead there is congestion, and they can alert us before we are even able to see the construction or the accident.

Mine typically says, "You're being rerouted due to traffic congestion ahead." I must admit I don't always follow the directions of my GPS when it decides to reroute, especially if I don't see the traffic that it is telling me is up ahead. Of course, if you are like me, after another several minutes, you will come to regret your decision because invariably, you'll run into stop-and-go traffic, or you'll have no ability to go at all.

We can draw a similar analogy to our spiritual lives and whose voice we are choosing to listen to. I heard a pastor years ago, and several others afterward, talk about spiritual GPS: *God's Positioning System*. We can think of hearing God's voice as listening to our spiritual GPS—our own internal detour navigator. I read a blog post written by Harold Herring called "7 Features Of Your God Given GPS." The features he pointed out were the following:

1) God's Positioning System
2) God's Possibility System
3) God's Protection System
4) God's Peace System
5) God's Promotion System
6) God's Power System
7) God's Prosperity System[17]

I love all the possibilities that he listed because they speak to the reasons it is crucial to be able to discern when God is speaking: protection, peace, promotion, prosperity, etc., and helps us to remember that we have access to His power and unlimited possibilities. Do I listen to the voice of the Holy Spirit as He directs me during a detour, or do I do things my own way? Do I doubt God's ability to see the future and His ability to have the best-laid plans for my life? Do I assume that I know more than God when it comes to leading me, and am I choosing to do it my way? Do I ignore all the warning signs? Do I ignore what I learned all the other times I chose to do my own things, and they led to disaster?

---

17 Harold Herring, "7 Features of Your God Given GPS," *Harold Herring*, https://haroldherring. com/276/.

THE DETOUR IS INTENTIONAL

So, as we walk toward our destiny, and we start experiencing trials and tribulations, we can choose to be obedient to our spiritual GPS. If we are listening to God's voice and following His direction when these detours happen, then we automatically start to look at them through the lens of Scripture. We know that with discernment and obedience, we will have protection.

In Exodus 3, God spoke to Moses through a burning bush. God told Moses that he was being sent to bring God's people out of Egypt. Now, Moses knew that he had heard God's voice, and after initially refusing to go, Moses was obedient. God had a specific task that I am sure Moses thought would be quick because it was a God-ordained task. However, God had other plans. We know that the Lord didn't just kill the Egyptians when He wanted Pharaoh to release the Israelites. Instead, God devised a strategy that would cause Him to get all the glory.

God allowed ten plagues to occur before Pharaoh had no choice but to release the Israelites. While God's plan was being wrought, the Israelites were still treated as slaves, and in Exodus 5, we are told that Pharaoh even further oppressed the Israelites. Even though they were in the process of being freed from slavery, it didn't seem that way. Even when they were protected from the plagues, their lives got harder before they got better.

I am sure they were wondering if Moses had truly heard God's voice. Moses didn't doubt, but he *was* upset with how God was having everything play out. In fact, Moses went back and complained to God, accused God of actually making trouble for the people, and asked this question:

"Why did you ever send me? Ever since I went into Pharoah to speak in your name he has caused trouble for this people, and you haven't rescued your people at all." —Exodus 5:22-23 (NASB)

We can learn a couple of things here about how we can and should react when we are sure that we have heard God's voice. First, Moses went back to God; he didn't doubt whose voice he heard, and he was authentic in his complaint to God. Secondly, he didn't allow others' doubts or anger to sway what he knew to be true: he had heard God. Often, the path that God provides, the detours that come, and how we react as a result may have others doubting our sanity and questioning if we truly heard from God.

We have to be like Moses and go back to the great I AM, making bold authentic statements to God. We don't need to converse with the doubting crowd because we know that eventually, what God promised will come to pass. Like Moses and so many Old Testament prophets, we must not be ashamed to be open and honest with God in our anger and frustration or in our rejoicing. God was doing what they didn't expect in their delivery to freedom. He had some detours He needed to make happen. So, Moses sought His voice again; even in anger, he sought His voice. The Israelites complained to Moses, and Moses went to God. It's a perfect example to us. As we go through hardships and when we know that we are hearing God's voice and being obedient, we can have real, authentic conversations with God and keep seeking His voice and His face when things happen that don't make sense.

The detours that God had planned persisted even after Pharaoh agreed to let God's people go, including God allowing them to go the longer way through the Red Sea. In the Bible, when we think of detours, we think of the people of Israel when they were being led by Moses out of captivity and through the wilderness. I watched a sermon recently titled "I Didn't Know We Were Going This Way" by Dr. Dharius Daniels. His text came from Exodus 13:17-18 (NIV):

When Pharaoh let the people go, God did not lead them on the road through the Philistine country, though that was shorter. For God said, "If they face war, they might change their minds and return to Egypt." So God led the people around by the desert road toward the Red Sea. The Israelites went out of Egypt ready for battle.

Because of Calvary, we are in a better situation now than the children of Israel were when they were being led to freedom out of Egypt. We don't need Moses in our lives.

Another aspect of our spiritual GPS is access to God's power. We always have the Holy Spirit with us, living on the inside of us. As we go through trials, we can remember that nothing is impossible for our God, and we have access to His obstacle-overcoming, resurrection-inducing, miracle-working power. I just need to make sure that as I discern that, I am obedient. As my relationship with God grows, matures, and becomes more intimate, it becomes easier to discern His voice, and I can be open and honest with God and explain my frustrations, my doubts, and my unbelief. (See Mark 9:23.)

I know that the Most High God, my heavenly Father, valued me so much that before I was formed, He had a plan that would allow me to have an intimate relationship with him—one in which I could call Him *Abba Father*. Jesus Himself spoke about discerning His voice and it being part of an intimate relationship with Him as our Good Shepherd. This relationship depends on my ability to hear His voice, know His voice, and, ultimately, follow Him. (See John 10:27.)

It was during a series of sermons over the last two years that I realized how hard the devil tries to thwart God's plan. I had so many moments throughout my life that I thought all my health issues were happening because of something I did. So, instead of listening to God's voice, I was listening to another voice—the voice of our adversary. The enemy's voice, at the time, was the loudest, and it kept saying, "See, God doesn't love you. God is punishing you." Instead, I should have been listening to God, whose voice was saying, "No, I'm upgrading you. I'm preparing you."

So, the key here is knowing the character of God and knowing that any doubt, negativity, fear, anxiety, hate, guilt, or shame is not of God. Right away, when those thoughts start to take root, we can flip the switch and turn up God's promises so that His voice is the only voice that we hear. Philippians 4:8-9 (NIV) tells us exactly how to do that:

> *Finally, brothers and sisters, whatever is true, whatever is noble, whatever is right, whatever is pure, whatever is lovely, whatever is admirable—if anything is excellent or praiseworthy—think about such things.*

God's purposes for our lives that He established for us before He created us in the secret place will be accomplished, no matter how hard the devil tries to get us to quit or fail. We can turn up the volume of God's Word so that we can withstand the darts of the enemy and tune out his lies and deception. That sermon series and Pastor Daniels's sermon were eye-opening for me. They caused me to have an aha moment because I started saying, "That's my line!" It could have been the title for several years of my life.

Anne Graham Lotz describes it perfectly:

I know the Lord is speaking to me personally when I read my Bible and a particular verse or passage seems illuminated—it just lifts up off the page, and I seem to hear a gentle, inaudible whisper as I have an "aha moment" in my heart.[18]

IIIIIIIIIIIIIIIIIIIIIIIIIIIIIIIIIIIIIIIIIIIIIIIIIIIIIIIIIIIIIIIIIIIIIIIIIIIIIIIIIIIIIIIIIIIIII

WE CAN TURN UP THE VOLUME OF GOD'S WORD SO THAT WE CAN WITHSTAND THE DARTS OF THE ENEMY AND TUNE OUT HIS LIES AND DECEPTION.

IIIIIIIIIIIIIIIIIIIIIIIIIIIIIIIIIIIIIIIIIIIIIIIIIIIIIIIIIIIIIIIIIIIIIIIIIIIIIIIIIIIIIIIIIIIIII

That happens so often for me, not just when I am doing my personal Bible study but also while I am in church or listening to a sermon online. I am sure we can all relate to certain things that happened in our lives that were so painful and seemed so unnecessary that we might say to God, like Dr. Daniels, "I didn't know we were going this way!" We remember Isaiah 55:8-9 talking about God's thoughts and ways not being ours. God sits on a different plane, and we really cannot even begin to grasp what we are called to obey—especially when we don't understand.

In the New Testament, before Jesus began His ministry, He fasted for forty days. The length of the fast is impressive enough, but in Matthew 4, we learn additionally that Jesus was in a desert

---

18 Priscilla Shirer quotes Anne Graham Lotz, *Discerning the Voice of God: How to Recognize When God Speaks* (Nashville, TN: LifeWay Press, 2017).

and—wait for it—the Holy Spirit led Him to that place. Maybe, we can say that it's easier to fast in a desert, but there was another catch. The Bible goes on to say that He was led for a specific purpose: "to be tempted by the devil" (Matthew 4:1, BSB).

Jesus was about to start His ministry, but God had a "detour" for Him. It went through the desert, so He could be tempted. Jesus is our Lord, our friend, and our big brother, and as Christians, one of our goals is to be more like Jesus. We are to use Jesus as our role model for how we are to live our lives and how we are to respond during difficulties—even those that the Spirit of God leads us through. So, we may not choose the assignments along the way to our destiny, but we can be certain that, like Jesus, we will be victorious because if we are purposefully following the Holy Spirit, we will grow from the hardships, and our lives will bring honor to God as we continue faithfully on the road to our God-ordained destiny

A. W. Tozer described it this way:

God will speak to the hearts of those who prepare themselves to hear, and conversely, those who do not so prepare themselves will hear nothing even though the Word of God is falling upon their outer ears every Sunday.[19]

THE DETOURS DEEPEN HIS VOICE

Earlier this year, I completed Priscilla Shirer's Bible study *Discerning the Voice of God: How to Recognize When God Speaks*. It was a true eye-opener. In this study, she talks about our ongoing alignment with Jesus Christ as a prerequisite to being able to discern God's voice throughout our lives. When our lives are

---

19 A. W. Tozer, *The Root of Righteousness* (Harrisburg, PA: Christian Publications, 1955).

aligned with Jesus Christ, as we face life's hardships and detours, and as we seek to hear and know God's voice, it will become clear, even during the storms. Knowing how to correctly discern God's voice will significantly reduce anxiety and stress.

Shirer outlined Five Ms of Correctly Hearing God:

1) Look for the message of the Spirit.

2) Live in the mode of prayer.

3) Search out the model of Scripture.

4) Submit to the ministry of Eli (wisdom).

5) Expect the mercy of confirmation.[20]

I want to expound on the five Ms that she says are the checks and balances that we need to help discern God's voice.

» In looking for the message of the Spirit, she talks about being intentional when listening to the Holy Spirit. Unfortunately (because we are a microwave society), this intentionality takes time, patience, and practice.

» We also need to live in the mode of prayer. By this, she means that before we speak to others about what is going on, our first communication should be with God.

» Thirdly, she admonishes us to check the Scriptures with what we are sensing God is saying to us: search out the model of Scripture. Does what we are hearing contradict God's character or His Word?

» The fourth item she mentions is that we ought to seek the counsel of a wise, more mature believer who is practiced in discerning God's voice. She calls this submitting to the ministry of Eli. She is referencing Samuel and Eli from 1 Samuel 3.

---

20 Priscilla Shirer, *Discerning the Voice of God: How to Recognize When God Speaks* (Nashville, TN: LifeWay Press, 2017) 33.

» Lastly, we are to expect the mercy of confirmation, which is basically asking the Lord to confirm what He has been saying to us internally with something external and tangible. God will always confirm for us through His Word, circumstances, and/or even through a person.

According to 1 Corinthians 14:33 (ESV), "God is not a God of confusion," and He wants to bring clarity to each situation. We need just ask and wait on Him.

God can speak through other saints, and that usually is one way that we can confirm what we may have already been hearing in our spirit from Him. Pastor Eric Petree's *Are We There Yet?* sermon series that I mentioned in the introduction truly was a life-changing series! It led to my decreased anxiety about missing God's voice. He stressed that we are born with a purpose. (See Jeremiah 1:5.) This fact was liberating to me because I believe that as children of God, He will help us to hear His voice to fulfill His plan. It also reminded me of another pastor, years ago when I lived in Georgia, who said something along the lines of, "God's ability to lead us is better than our ability to miss His lead." It was a mind-blowing, eye-opening, mouth-gaping statement, followed by hand-raising and clapping and just worshiping.

Pastor Eric also preached a sermon on alignment in which he spoke primarily about the earthly company that we keep and making sure that they didn't derail us. Instead, we ought to align with those who can encourage us and help us fulfill our destiny. Our company should help us as we seek to hear God's voice and be obedient to His calling. We also know ultimately that we must, first and foremost, align ourselves with Jesus Christ.

The Lord used Pastor Eric's ministry of Eli to, once again, speak to my heart about writing this book. I understood that I was so loved that God had my purpose first and then created me. I will always remember him saying and having us repeat with such fervor: "I am not an accident! I was created on purpose for a purpose! And I will fulfill that purpose and get to my destiny."

DON'T HOPE TO HEAR—EXPECT TO HEAR!

So, as we walk on the path, as Pastor Eric Petree says, from purpose to destiny, we need to have checks and balances in place to keep us on the path. We need to make sure that whether by our own folly and sin or under the Lord's guidance, we don't allow detours to derail us completely from getting to destiny. Charles R. Swindoll put it like this:

> *God makes His desires known to those who stop at His Word look in, with a sensitive spirit, and listen to others. When we go to His Word, we stop long enough to hear from above. When we look, we examine our surrounding circumstances in light of what He is saying to our inner spirit (perhaps you prefer to call this your conscience) and when we listen to others, we seek the counsel of wise, qualified people.*[21]

In his book *The Will of God: Understanding and Pursuing His Ultimate Plan for Your Life*, Charles Stanley eloquently spoke about several key factors in discerning God's will. A key part of discerning God's voice is knowing that God wants to reveal Himself to us and promises to show us His will: "Decide right now to believe this simple fact—*your Savior wants you to know*

---

21 Charles R. Swindoll, *Stress Fractures* (Grand Rapids, MI: Zondervan, 1994).

His will so you can walk in it."[22] So, as we all strive to discern God's voice in our lives—as we make big and small decisions—know that God is not trying to make it difficult for us to hear His voice. Friends, He wants us to succeed. Stanley put it this way, "It is God's character to reveal His will to you."[23]

In Psalm 32:8 (NASB), we are told the following: "I will instruct you and teach you in the way which you should go; I will counsel you with My eye upon you." I especially love this scripture because it tells us that God has His eyes on us. As we strive to discern what He is saying to us, if His eyes are on us, He will help us as we navigate life's detours. Another key that Charles Stanley pointed out was the fact that "God promises to show you His will."[24] And we all know that if God made a promise, He is not a man that He would lie. (See Numbers 23:19.) So we know that He will do what He promised He would do.

Earlier in the chapter, we discussed the 5 Ms of discerning God's voice; however, also important is realizing that God will use our daily circumstances. He can speak to us through even the mundane portions of our lives. Oswald Chambers, in his book *My Utmost for His Highest,* more eloquently stated this point:

We can all see God in exceptional things, but it requires the growth of spiritual discipline to see God in every detail. Never believe that the so-called random events of life are anything less than God's appointed order. Be ready to discover His divine designs anywhere and everywhere.[25]

---

22 Charles F. Stanley, *The Will Of God: Understanding And Pursuing His Ultimate Plan For Your Life* (New York, NY: Howard Books, 2020).
23 Charles F. Stanley, *The Will Of God.*
24 Charles F. Stanley, *The Will Of God.*
25 Oswald Chambers, *My Utmost for His Highest: The Classic Daily Devotional* (Uhrichsville, OH: Barbour Books, 2015).

Along the path of discernment, we should remember, as Stanley stated in *The Will of God: Understanding and Pursuing His Ultimate Plan for your Life*:

> *He orchestrates everything you need—moving people, resources, situations and even changing you—all to carry out His wonderful will for your life. Even the struggles you are experiencing today He is communicating through—engineering the details, limits and solutions that concern you—all to prepare you to walk in His purposes for your life.[26]*

This should take some of the stress off as we realize that we are not alone in searching out His voice. Charles Stanley goes further to say:

> *So you don't have to be afraid about missing God's will or misinterpreting what He is trying to say. You also don't have to worry about accomplishing His plan once He reveals it to you. The Lord God is able to speak to you clearly and empower you to do whatever He calls you to do.[27]*

What does that mean for us today? Simply that at the appropriate times, God will give the necessary instructions to make His plan come to fruition. Key to making sure we are able to hear from God and discern His voice is making sure we spend time in His Word and communicate with Him in prayer—talking and listening.

Some hindrances to discerning/hearing God's voice, according to Charles Stanley, include ignorance of God's character and principles, unbelief, feelings of unworthiness or guilt, busyness, God-directed anger, and willfully harbored sin.[28] If you are like

---

26 Charles F. Stanley, *The Will Of God*.
27 Charles F. Stanley, *The Will Of God*.
28 Charles F. Stanley, *The Will Of God*.

me, you may have nodded your head as you read this list since there is at least one thing with which you can associate personally as a possible hindrance. We must allow the Holy Spirit to reveal the hindrance and to help us turn away from it so that discerning can become much easier for us.

||||||||||||||||||||||||||||||||||||||||||||||||||||||||||||||||||||||||||||||||||||||||||||||

WE MUST ALLOW THE HOLY SPIRIT TO REVEAL THE HINDRANCE AND TO HELP US TURN AWAY FROM IT SO THAT DISCERNING CAN BECOME MUCH EASIER FOR US.

||||||||||||||||||||||||||||||||||||||||||||||||||||||||||||||||||||||||||||||||||||||||||||||

Now, unlike twenty years ago, I do better when trying to unpack detours and discerning what God is saying to me and wanting me to learn during these detours. What exactly does this mean currently in my life? What is God's Word saying? What is God saying? Do I have a trusted, mature believer who knows how to discern God's voice and to whom I can talk about things after I have discussed them with God? Can and do I have the patience to wait on His confirmation before acting on impulse and doing what I believe to be true versus waiting on and acting on what I know to be true because I heard from God?

I recently read a quote from R. T. Kendall who stated it like this: "It takes greater faith and devotion to pray, trust, and obey when God is absent than when He is present."[29] I would make a minor adjustment to this statement. I would only say that God is never absent; it is just our perception when he is silent. It is hard to trust when we are waiting, and it seems that God isn't speaking, but I would also say that He is never silent, just as He is never absent. I can now so clearly see how when God wasn't answering my biggest questions, He was blessing me still. He was still showing up in situations I wasn't asking Him directly to intervene in, and His answer was, "I have you in the palm of my hands. You are safe here, and you will be blessed. You will have an abundant life not as the world sees it but as I the Lord see it!"

In many ways, discerning His voice is being able to hear when He is not only speaking but when He is whispering. It is the "still, small voice" (1 Kings 19:12, BSB).

---

29 R. T. Kendall, *The Sensitivity of the Spirit: Learning to Stay in the Flow of God's Direction* (Lake Mary, FL: Charisma House, 2002).

CHAPTER 4

Accepting God's Will

"I cry out to God Most High, to God who fulfills His purpose for me."
—Psalm 57:2 (BSB)

In the last chapter, I wrote about being able to discern God's voice. I also mentioned being obedient to his voice. It may seem like second nature to assume that if we are being obedient that we have accepted His will for our lives. However, that may not be the case. So in this chapter, we will talk about how important it is to accept God's will—especially when it doesn't make sense to us, the way is not clear, and things seem to be confusing or just plain difficult.

Part of accepting God's will is laying down our rights and our desires and picking up His will and trusting what God is doing. It truly is an example of the crucified life described in Galatians 2:20 (KJV): "I am crucified with Christ: nevertheless I live; yet not I, but Christ liveth in me: and the life which I now live in the flesh I live by the faith of the Son of God." I love A. W. Tozer's definition from his book of the same title, *The Crucified Life*. He said it is "a life wholly given over to the Lord in absolute humility, and obedience: a sacrifice pleasing to the Lord."[30]

PART OF ACCEPTING GOD'S WILL IS LAYING DOWN OUR RIGHTS AND OUR DESIRES AND PICKING UP HIS WILL AND TRUSTING WHAT GOD IS DOING.

---

30 A. W. Tozer and James L. Snyder, *The Crucified Life: How to Live out a Deeper Christian Experience* (Minneapolis, MN: Bethany House, 2014).

It is hard at times to accept God's will because we sometimes believe that God is always going to ask something hard of us like moving to Africa to be a missionary in the jungles, or we believe He will insist that we live a life devoid of fun. It seems like an oxymoron to say crucified life, but it is dying to our own will that we encounter real life. Tozer went on:

If a life is truly crucified, it is dead and not alive. But how can a person be dead and alive at the same time? Being dead and yet alive is one of the strange inconsistencies of the life established for us by Jesus' dying on the cross. But oh, the blessedness of these seeming inconsistencies.[31]

We can think of several instances in the Bible in which we see the people of God accepting God's will when it seemed impossible, even though they didn't always *willingly* accept it. In Genesis 6, Noah agreed with God's plan to build an ark to withstand a flood when those around doubted it. Sarah laughed at God when He revealed His plan for her and Abraham to have children in their old age in Genesis 18. Abraham took his only son, as commanded by God, to be sacrificed because He believed God would provide another animal as we see in Genesis 22:5 (NIV, emphasis added) when Abraham said, "Stay here with the donkey while I and the boy go over there. We will worship and then *we* will come back to you." Abraham trusted God with the life of His son. He had to have remembered the promise God had made to him back in Genesis 15:5 and knew that the descendants He was talking about would not be from another child. He tried that (Ishmael) and already knew another son was not God's plan.

---

31 A. W. Tozer and James L. Snyder, *The Crucified Life*.

Like Abraham, you and I have to always remember God's promises, His character, and His love for us and trust His every direction for every step that we take once we allow Him to have the reins of our lives. That is how accepting God's will becomes easier for us when we start to live the crucified life. During the quiet times with God, when we are being downloaded with information, we must develop trust because part of accepting God's will is trusting that He knows best and that He only has our best in mind. (See Psalm 84:11 and James 1:7.)

God rarely gives us step-by-step directions, and we are not warned like our GPS in the car often does during a road trip of upcoming detours. We know God longs to reveal Himself and His will for our lives, but the how comes as we step out in faith, trusting Him as we walk. Charles Stanley had another reason why it is important that we accept His will:

The Lord cares about the choice that is weighing on your mind, His greater goal is to deepen your relationship with Him. So, He doesn't just want to answer a question in your heart; rather, He wants to form a pattern for you to relate to Him in every aspect of your life. He desires for you to be continuously aware of His goal for you, the ways He speaks to you, what may be hindering His will, and how you can confirm His path for you.[32]

HIS GLORY IS OUR INCENTIVE!

The Lord requires full obedience once He has revealed His will—not partial obedience, but full obedience, even when we would choose the exact opposite scenario. In the book of Daniel, we are well acquainted with the story of the three Hebrew boys

32 Charles Stanley, *The Will of God.*

who were thrown in a very hot furnace. Shadrach, Meshach, and Abednego were friends of Daniel. King Nebuchadnezzar had them thrown in the fiery furnace because they refused to bow down to the golden image of the king.

The ultimate example of accepting God's will was evident in the lives of these Hebrew boys. Even though they were threatened with sure death, they chose to follow God's commands which clearly stated that they were not to worship any idols. They demonstrated true obedience and surrender and then, later, had the supreme revelation of a fourth man in the fire with them. A. W. Tozer let us know that as we accept God's will, "We do not need to know the outcome in order to obey God. As a matter of faith and trust, we obey God simply because He is God. This obedience brings us to a point of a personal resolution where we do not have to be delivered from our trouble."[33]

It is important to also realize that troubles can be one means by which God gets the glory, so we accept the good and bad as it could all be part of God's divine will for our lives. Shadrach, Meshach, and Abednego surrendered to their fate. In a come-what-may scenario, they were going to be loyal to God to the bitter end. So, we know we should surrender to His will so that when "repudiating the situation is the order of the day—we must never confuse that with an opportunity to surrender in such a way that we get out of God's way and allow Him to do in us what He wants to do through us.[34]

The final stage of the crucified life, and I believe one of the main reasons we should always accept God's will is that it leads

---

33 Charles Stanley, *The Will of God*.
34 A. W. Tozer, *The Crucified Life*.

to a revelation of God in our lives and the lives of those around us in a spectacular way:

> *Then King Nebuchadnezzar was astonished; and he rose in haste and spoke, saying to his counselors, "Did we not cast three men bound into the midst of the fire?"*
>
> *They answered and said to the king, "True, O king."*
>
> *"Look!" he answered, "I see four men loose, walking in the midst of the fire; and they are not hurt, and the form of the fourth is like the Son of God."* —Daniel 3:24-25 (NKJV)

So, surely, the rhetorical question is this. Do we want to experience such a vast revelation of God in our life?

> *"Oh, see that fourth man in the flame!" That is the revelation of God. What does it take to experience God in this way? It takes a furnace. It takes obedience to God and submitting to Him in absolute surrender. That is all.*[35]

It can take spectacular life experiences for us to get big mountaintop revelations of God our Father and to experience His presence in tangible ways. We all are aware that God is omnipresent—that is, He is everywhere all at once and can exist without our awareness. However, accepting and surrendering to God's will in our lives will lead to His manifest presence and, as referenced in the Old Testament, as the *Shekinah* (dwelling/settling) glory of God. Acceptance will lead to God's manifest presence—Him in sweet fellowship with us, His creation, dwelling with us, settling in with us even in the midst of our furnaces. In the midst of our own burning bushes, we can also be standing on *holy ground.*

We can concur with A.W. Tozer:

---

35 A. W. Tozer, *The Crucified Life.*

God's most delicate tools are reserved for His special children. For
the Christian on the path of the crucified life, God will bring into
his pathway the fiery furnace, the Refiner's Fire, and show that
Christian how much He really loves him.[36]

REMEMBRANCE: A ROUTE TO ACCEPTANCE

We can learn the benefits of accepting God's will over time, and
by this, I mean that each time we accept God's will, we build up
a memory bank of the blessedness that ensued just because we
surrendered. Charles Stanley described it this way:

Once you truly hear His voice and experience what it's like to
walk in His will, you won't want to live any other way. So don't
fight Him. Seek Him, submit to Him, and watch Him make
more of your life than you ever imagined possible.[37]

I would say that the diagnosis of systemic lupus erythematous
during medical school started what I call my medical wilderness, and with each medical trial, I needed to remember God's
faithfulness through the prior season because, in each wilderness,
there is an oasis.

In the geographical sense, an oasis is an otherwise dry and arid
region made fertile by a source of fresh water. Oases (more than
one oasis) are irrigated by natural springs or other underground
water sources, and they tend to vary in size. Did you know that an
oasis can yield crops? Common oasis crops include dates, cotton,
olives, figs, citrus fruits, wheat, and corn. So, even in our wilderness seasons, we can be fruitful and still live a life that glorifies
God and give witness to His protection of His children.

---

36 A. W. Tozer, *The Crucified Life.*
37 Charles Stanley, *The Will of God.*

I am reminded of the numerous times in the Old Testament that Israel is referred to as "a land flowing with milk and honey." It was a reminder to the Israelites of God's providence. Surprisingly to me and maybe to some of you, Israel has its greatest regions dominated by the Negev desert in the south. It occupies more than half of the country's total land area! Yes, so as we go through wilderness experiences, we can use them as a reminder to us that with God, nothing is impossible. He can make a country that is predominantly a desert into a land flowing with milk and honey and a reminder that we need not fear because our God "will supply all your needs according to His riches in glory in Christ Jesus" (Philippians 4:19, NIV).

So, no matter the diagnosis, as I take the treatment and have the necessary blood tests and imaging, I still trust and believe God for my healing. I keep looking at the horizon, not for a mirage but for the author and finisher of my faith, Christ Jesus. Each time I remember how the Holy Spirit was my aide, confidante, healer, companion, and friend, I remember that Jesus said, rivers of living water will flow from the innermost being of those who believe in Him. Therefore, when I ruptured my colon in 2004, I remembered how the rheumatologist, several years earlier when I was first diagnosed with SLE, didn't think I should continue in medical school.

However, as I was healing from the ruptured colon with a colostomy bag, I was also preparing to start my first job as a neurologist. If God got me through that, surely He could do the same now and then in 2019 as I was once again hospitalized but now because of urosepsis. I had been through enough of my medical wilderness to know He could do it again. It becomes easier each time to accept the wilderness experiences because in them, we have oases. We become refined, and the size of our oases enlarges as it becomes easier to accept His will for our lives.

The sudden death of my mother and then, two years later, the death of my grandmother have taught me that we may have plans, but ultimately, as children of the Most High God, we have to accept His will for our lives and those of our loved ones. To discern God's will, we must already be striving to obey whatever God has commanded in His Scriptures. That requires us to be well-learned students of the written Word of God because we cannot obey what we do not know.

Throughout my life, God has allowed things to happen and called me to do things that have developed my faith, deepened my trust in Him, and fostered a more intimate relationship. As you have noticed already from reading my story so far, I didn't always respond the right way immediately, and God was gracious. Each time I missed the mark or didn't learn the lesson that was being taught, the Lord continued the process until I learned what He needed me to learn; sometimes, the lesson had to be relearned and relearned again.

I also learned that partial obedience is disobedience, and *sort of* obeying God but doing what I wanted to do all along doesn't work in God's kingdom. Pastor Steve J. Cole preached a sermon in September 2013 titled "The Peril of Partial Obedience." It was based on the story of Rehoboam in 2 Chronicles 10-12. He mentioned that partial obedience can often look like planning first, praying second, and asking God to bless the plan I have formulated—instead of seeking Him first, doing as HE directs, and submitting to God's Word.

||||||||||||||||||||||||||||||||||||||||||||||||||||||||||||||||||||||||||||||||||||||||||

THROUGHOUT MY LIFE, GOD HAS ALLOWED THINGS TO HAPPEN AND CALLED ME TO DO THINGS THAT HAVE DEVELOPED MY FAITH, DEEPENED MY TRUST IN HIM, AND FOSTERED A MORE INTIMATE RELATIONSHIP.

||||||||||||||||||||||||||||||||||||||||||||||||||||||||||||||||||||||||||||||||||||||||||

It can also mean following God when in need but forsaking Him when we are doing well. He termed it foxhole faith: "You cry out to God when you're in a jam but forget Him when things are going well." Partial obedience will lead to partial or no blessings and always has built-in consequences. Some of the consequences of partial obedience that he highlighted in his sermon are continual hassles and being in the service of a more difficult master:

> God loves you; the world couldn't care less about you. God seeks to build you as a person; the world tears you down. God gives your life purpose by fitting [it] into His eternal plan; the world has no purpose except trying to make yourself happy for a few years before you die. Would you rather serve the Lord or the world?

If we are continually experiencing unease, no rest, or no peace, it could be from partial disobedience. It could also be God's way of making us more like Jesus. So, as we go through life, we must take inventory of our lives and our responses to God's laws and directives.

Pastor Cole offered three solutions to partial obedience:

1) See the foolishness of trying to dodge God.

2) Humble yourself and acknowledge God's righteousness in disciplining you through trials.

3) Set your heart to seek God.

I realized with time that after each trial, my trust in Him grew, my response became one of dependence and total obedience, and I developed a posture of resoluteness, obedience, thankfulness, and expectancy! Setting one's heart implies a deliberate, sustained focus. You don't accidentally or casually fall into seeking the Lord. You have to resolve to seek God through His Word and prayer and obey His commands.

I have also learned the value of short prayers:

» "Lord, I believe; help my unbelief!" (Mark 9:24, NKJV)

» "Lord, help me." (Matthew 15:25, NIV)

» "God, have mercy on me, a sinner!" (Luke 18:13, BSB)

» "By His stripes I am healed." (Isaiah 53:5, author paraphrase)

» "Oh, that you would bless me and enlarge my territory! Let your hand be with me and keep me from harm so that I will be free from pain." (1 Chronicles 4:10, NIV)

» "There is none holy like the LORD: for there is none besides You; there is no rock like our God." (1 Samuel 2:2, ESV)

As we learn to set our hearts to seek God in all that we do or think, it becomes easier to be obedient. Faith in God means putting our trust in God. As our faith grows through trials, our total obedience to God will grow. The result is righteousness.

Trust is truly a two-way street. We tend to focus a lot on trusting God. But guess what? We should all want God to be able to trust us! This lesson is demonstrated by the parable of the talents found in Matthew 25:14-30 and Luke 19:11-27. Having

God trust us depends on our trust in Him. David A. DePra, in an article titled "Can God Trust Us?" says:

> *The irony is that the way in which we become trustworthy to God is by trusting Him. Indeed, unconditional faith in God is the only way in which we can become those whom God can trust. For it is only if all that I have, indeed, all that I am, has been relinquished into the hands of God by faith, that I can be trusted with those things.[38]*

And you know that I decided to write this book only after being challenged by Pastor Eric Petree and prodded by my aunt Andrea. After I accepted the task and decided to walk in full obedience, I started to realize that it was God trusting me to bring glory to His name on a larger national scale, not just my "Jerusalem." (See Acts 1:8.) Pastor Eric's "Cut the Bologna" and "No Excuses" messages resonated with me. I realized that God had called me to other things, but I was limiting myself because of my insecurities—and to be honest, my laziness.

When I spoke with my publisher about this project, two of them said to me on different occasions, "If God has placed it in your heart to write this book, then He already has the audience." So, I had to trust the call, the process, and the result to Him because God was in it. God is the architect of our lives. He places His will inside of us, and as we accept the plan, we also must work to execute it so that His will ultimately is accomplished through us. I want to be a part of God's redemption story, and I don't want someone else doing what I was created to do. As Pastor Eric has said on multiple occasions, God has a purpose, and He's decided that [insert your name] will accomplish it.

---

38 David A. DePra, "Can God Trust Us?" *God Trust Us*, www.goodnewsarticles.com/Jul05-2.htm.

I started going to Citygate Church after the COVID-19 pandemic of 2020. Many bad things happened because of the pandemic, but I am grateful it brought me to Citygate Church. I am sure the Lord could have used other means to get me to that church, but that was the vehicle He used. Despite what it may look like in the natural, our heavenly Father is always orchestrating things for our good. His will is always bigger and better than what we would have wanted. And He builds His church and places us in a specific church to accomplish His will for our lives but also for the church as a body.

KNOW YOUR ENEMY

Our adversary, the devil, is a roaring lion constantly prowling, seeking whom he can devour. Trials and hardships come, but if we stay resolute in our pursuit of Christ, we can and will accomplish God's will. The big why I had through so many of my trials was finally answered. In the past, I would often see trials and disappointment as "Marsha is a failure," "Marsha is not enough," "Marsha is being punished," or "Marsha is not loved." The devil knows that if I was created, it naturally meant that God has a great purpose for my life.

Therefore, the adversary plans to thwart God's plan by any means necessary. He has no real power, but he believes if he can keep me or us from manifesting our destiny, then the battle he is fighting would be won. He's lost the war, but he is still trying to win small battles. One of the ways he succeeds is by keeping us feeling defeated, unloved, and isolated.

In the book of Job, the devil's knowledge about the hedge of protection God had around Job tells us a couple of things: The devil must have tried before to get to Job and realized he couldn't because of the hedge of protection. And God has a hedge of protection around His children. We can take solace in that we are eternally surrounded by God's protection. Each time something comes to us in this life, we can know that we are protected, and nothing is coming to us that God and we can't handle together.

It was life-changing when I realized that some of my trials could indicate that the devil was on a mission to derail God's plan, and it changed my mindset as trials have come along. I now know that I must recognize the lies as the devil's tool because God's plan for our lives, if we live surrendered to Him, is not optional.

||||||||||||||||||||||||||||||||||||||||||||||||||||||||||||||||||||||||||||||||||||||||||||||

WE ALL HAVE DREAMS AND DESIRES FOR OUR LIVES. I BELIEVE THAT THERE ARE TIMES WHEN WHAT WE CONSIDER TO BE OUR DREAMS AND DESIRES ARE IN FACT GOD'S.

||||||||||||||||||||||||||||||||||||||||||||||||||||||||||||||||||||||||||||||||||||||||||||||

We all have dreams and desires for our lives. I believe that there are times when what *we* consider to be *our* dreams and desires are in fact *God's*. When Psalm 37:4 says that if we delight ourselves in God, He will give us the desires of our heart, that scripture comes alive in my life. If you are like me, at some point or another, you thought that it meant that if you were serving and surrendered to God, then God would grant you anything you want in life.

It really doesn't. Instead, it means that a surrendered life leads to God making *His* plans and will for our lives, *our* dreams, and desires for *ourselves*.

Beth Moore, published Christian author and Bible teacher, says, "Often when God does not readily give us what we want, it is because He knows what our desire would cost us. Faith sometimes means forgoing our desires because we trust Christ to have a better plan for our lives."[39] Even though He has placed those desires within us, we do have to work at them to get them accomplished. We must build our lives with the tools He will provide. When we receive that word, we can ignore the enemy and focus on walking in the path the Holy Spirit has revealed to us and not be distracted, weary, and discouraged.

Discouragement can be a normal stage that we go through, but it should never become a state that we are stuck in. If we remain distracted, weary, and discouraged, it affects the way we go about accomplishing God's will. Once we know His will, we must ask God to give us the strength and fortitude so that we can build and battle at the same time.

HIS GOODNESS REVEALED THROUGH OUR WEAKNESSES

Psalm 27:13 (KJV) says, "*I had fainted*, unless I had believed to see the goodness of the Lord in the land of the living." We are apt to be faint, weary, and weak—especially as we go through one struggle after another. For me, it was one medical diagnosis after another. I must admit that I often wondered if the doctor was right, and maybe I should have chosen another career. The

39 Beth Moore, *A Heart like His* (Nashville, TN: Broadman & Holman, 1999).

ensuing years gradually got worse as I had joint pains, skin rash, muscle aches, chronic fatigue, depression, insomnia, and eventually kidney damage, heart inflammation, and weight gain.

At times, I was overwhelmed by it all, and it was hard on so many days for me to accept that this was my life. I felt like I never got a chance to just breathe before I was confronted with another trial. I didn't understand. I was trying to "do the right thing." I was doing what I thought was God's plan for my life. Why He would allow so much pain and suffering was beyond me. Why did it have to be so difficult to get through medical school when I knew there were other students who weren't Christians, and they were getting along—in my estimation—"just fine."

I can see now that, as a result of what I went through, I am more empathetic with each of my patients. I may not have the same diagnosis, but I can relate in ways that someone who hasn't had health issues wouldn't be able to. Like Joseph, many of us can say our own version of Genesis 50:20 and should be able to say, "What was meant for evil, God meant it unto good for us but also to bring about His plans."

We have often heard it said that if the devil knew what Jesus would accomplish in the tomb, he would have worked hard to prevent the crucifixion. We often cry on Good Friday and rejoice on Easter Sunday, but our eternity with God wouldn't be secure if there weren't a Saturday—not for rest but for deliverance. In Colossians 2:15, we are told that He disarmed the powers and authorities, making a public spectacle of them and ultimately triumphing over them by the cross, and in Revelation, Jesus reminds us that He arose with the keys of death and hades. The devil ultimately is defeated, and we need to live our lives from a stance of VICTORY and acceptance of what God has for us.

In medical school and during my neurology residency, there were days I felt like giving up. I also worried that I would flunk out. Despite the constant interruptions of treatment and the chronic fatigue and insomnia associated with my illness, I never asked for and was never given special consideration. Many days, I thought I was alone, enduring punishment for things that I wasn't even sure what I had done, but it was "my cross to bear." I was able to complete medical school without requiring extra time. Somehow, through pleuritis (inflammation of the lining of the lung) and later, also developing what was finally diagnosed as pericarditis (inflammation of the heart), I just kept going. At the time, I wasn't sure how, but I did.

And with each hardship and trial, I learned how to trust God more and to accept His will for my life. It became easier to trust His sovereignty in all other areas of my life as well, through the good and the bad. It is when we are weak and humble before God that He is able to accomplish the impossible in our lives, and if we are patient, the impossible will be bigger and better than any dream we could have tried to imagine on our own.

The apostle Paul put it like this in 2 Corinthians 12:6-10 (CSB):

For if I want to boast, I wouldn't be a fool, because I would be telling the truth. But I will spare you, so that no one can credit me with something beyond what he sees in me or hears from me, especially because of the extraordinary revelations. Therefore, so that I would not exalt myself, a thorn in the flesh was given to me, a messenger of Satan to torment me so that I would not exalt myself. Concerning this I pleaded with the Lord three times that it would leave me. But he said to me, "My grace is sufficient for you, for my power is perfected in weakness."

Therefore, I will most gladly boast all the more about my weaknesses, so that Christ's power may reside in me. So I take pleasure in weaknesses, insults, hardships, persecutions, and in difficulties, for the sake of Christ. For when I am weak, then I am strong.

I know without a doubt that it was a praying mother and grandmother that got me through those days and that has helped me to keep going, providing strength and enabling me to keep pursuing God's will for my life. I wouldn't have been able to personalize words like Jeremiah 1:5 and say, "God chose me, and He formed me in my mother's womb and set me apart to be a physician." He chose me! We are told in Hebrews that the Bible is alive and active, and for me, that means I can personalize it to my life for various seasons and situations so that it can do the work God means for it to do. You can too.

Another one of my favorite scriptures that helped me through medical school is found in Psalm 139:13-16. Here, David talked about how God created him; he was fearfully and wonderfully made. It became a favorite because of the insecurities that I also suffered throughout that time. Despite the illnesses, I was fearfully and wonderfully made by the heavenly Father. He also ordained all of my days before they came to be.

As we go through our daily walk in what we have perceived to be God's plan for our lives, we have to constantly remind ourselves that as we walk in His will—despite what may come—we are walking the path that He has ordained for us. Knowing that the author and finisher of our faith has our lives in His hands and will accomplish His will should bring us comfort, allow us to endure the trials, and permit our faith to grow.

Psalm 139 and the verse about being fearfully and wonderfully made has such a special place in my heart also because I was born out of wedlock. I've felt like an accident for most of my life. I even went as far as to believe that because of that, I had less purpose. I myself was less than. My mom was also born out of wedlock, so at times, it would magnify my perception that I was less than because my mother *and* I had less-than-stellar births. That verse is a reminder to me that I was no accident in God's eye; I wasn't a surprise for Him.

He knitted me together in my mother's womb. I do not know how to knit, but I know that it is laborious and time-consuming, but when done properly, it produces masterpieces. My God does nothing short of creating masterpieces. Psalm 139 helps me to realize how much love God had for me even before my mom knew me. I have a purpose, and I am a part of God's divine plan. My purpose was there before I even came to be like He said in Jeremiah. Those words scream, "I love you!" Even the difficult times are part of God's plan for my life.

Accepting God's will included near-death experiences. Once again, I had to choose how I would survive that season. Would I just exist, or would I find a way to thrive? In the summer of 2004, right before I ruptured my colon and almost died, I was on a high. I was finishing my movement disorder fellowship training at Emory, about to start a new job that July, and had just bought my very first home. Everything was going great in my life, and then the huge setback.

But I learned a lot during that season, and one thing was to trust that inner voice. I know it was the voice of the Holy Spirit. His voice prompted me to make the call that Monday morning that ultimately led to me having emergency surgery at the end of that day. I know that God wasn't finished with me and had more for me to do, and that is why I survived that ordeal. Even though for three months I had to change a colostomy bag and I worried about the bag having an odor, especially when I went back to work, God was still at work.

I relied a lot on praise music, prayers, and family support during that time. Byron Cage, whom I incidentally saw at New Birth Missionary Baptist Church, had a few songs come out between 2003 and 2005 that were so encouraging to me on some of my worse days. I'd like to briefly mention some that helped to alleviate the depression and discouragement: "The Presence of the Lord Is Here," "Glory to Your Name," "I Will Bless the Lord," and "Broken But I'm Healed."

HIS WILL ADVANCES US

Accepting God's will for our lives doesn't always mean that there will be no trials. In some ways, it may mean that there will be more battles to face. As mentioned previously, because our adversary wants to derail God's plan, he will be trying harder as we walk in God's will.

Paul said in Colossians 3:23-24 (ESV), "Whatever you do, work heartily, as for the Lord and not for men, knowing that from the Lord you will receive the inheritance as your reward. You are serving the Lord Christ." Depending on the season of life that we are in, we must look at the Scriptures differently. Sometimes, we learn different things from them. I can now look at that scripture and realize that as I accept and walk in God's will, I am working for the Lord, and greater than my paycheck is the fact that I also will have an eternal inheritance.

The devil will try to poison our thought life with his lies. It is one of his main weapons to thwart God's will. The battles we wage against the principalities, powers, rulers of the darkness, and against spiritual wickedness in high places are exactly why we need to ensure that we are walking in God's will. We need the full backing of heaven as we soldier on toward our destiny. We are soldiers in God's army, and we can run straight toward our enemy in full assurance that God's will is being accomplished through the help of the Holy Spirit living within us.

Each battle that we fight and win advances us not just in earthly blessings but also in kingdom blessings. We, like Timothy, can say:

I have fought the good fight, I have finished the race, I have kept the faith. There is reserved for me the crown of righteousness, which the Lord, the righteous Judge, will give me on that day, and not only to me, but to all those who have loved his appearing.
—2 Timothy 4:7–8 (NIV)

And Beth Moore, one of my favorite women's Bible teachers, says:

God surpasses our dreams when we reach past our personal plans and agenda to grab the hand of Christ and walk the path He chose for us. He is obligated to keep us dissatisfied until we come to him and his plans for complete satisfaction.[40]

---

40 Beth Moore and Dale McCleskey, *Breaking Free: Making Liberty in Christ a Reality in Life* (Nashville, TN: Broadman & Holman, 2000).

It is only when we surrender our personal agendas and dreams and grab hold of God's perfect plan and desires for our lives that we can have satisfaction in life and live the exceedingly abundant life!

CHAPTER 5

Overcoming Hardships

"These things I have spoken unto you, that in me ye might have peace. In the world ye shall have tribulation: but be of good cheer; I have overcome the world."
—John 16:33 (KJV)

Many of us when we have read or heard about hardships it is usually associated with another word: enduring. I thought about naming this chapter "Enduring Hardships" but decided against it because for me, enduring seems to have such a negative connotation. If I think that I am enduring something, I feel as if I am barely surviving. It makes me feel that there is no way out of the present circumstance; I must hunker down until it is over. So, I decided to look up the definition of the two words: enduring and overcoming.

Enduring, in the *Collins English Dictionary* means, "permanent; lasting."[41] The definition of overcoming is "to get the better of in a struggle or conflict, conquer, defeat."[42] Right away, we can see that there is a profound difference in the meanings, and I believe, in how I view my hardships in the past and in the future. I can see that just by framing our hardships as something we can and will overcome, we already have a different mindset, and that will shape and determine how we go through the hardship. I can go through faith-filled and assured of the outcome that will be for my good. I may not be happy about it, but I can still be praising God despite the hardships. I know that what is happening is not permanent, I will win, and I can come out of it a victor and not a victim. I also now know that if the result is something as permanent as death, with His help, I can still be an overcomer.

Some hardships can be viewed as divine intervention or inter-ruptions. In *Life Interrupted*, by Priscilla Shirer, she breaks it down

---

41 "Enduring Definition and Meaning: Collins English Dictionary," *Collins*, https://www.collinsdictionary.com/us/dictionary/english/ enduring#:~:text=(%C9%AAn%CB%88dj%CA%8A%C9%99r%C9%AA%C5%8B%20)-,adjective,having%20forbearance%3B%20long%2Dsuffering.
42 "Overcome Definition and Meaning: Collins English Dictionary," *Collins*, https://www.collinsdictionary.com/us/dictionary/english/overcome.

simply: Divine Intervention + Yielded Submission = Eternal Significance.[43] She says:

> *We're here to tell God's story. And none of us are too good, too cultured, too Christianized, or too impressive for Him to thread any plotline He desires through our lives, even if that plotline has a destination like Nineveh in it.*[44]

I can be an overcomer if I realize that because God is in it, there is eternal significance in every aspect of my life. As an overcomer, and because we are His sons and daughters, we realize that God's providence is at work in the midst of every good and perfect gift, but more importantly, it is also at work in our hardships.

Can we become overcomers? Are there ways that we qualify to be overcomers? I would say a resounding, yes and yes! We cannot be overcomers if we have nothing to overcome. We have to allow hardships, but not only that, we have to embrace the hardships. Remember: we will be in a battle, a spiritual battle, so I encourage you to be prepared to fight. Fight like your life depends on it because it does!

As Christians, we have been born again, and in this new birth, God has equipped us to be overcomers. We have to take hold of that which He has given us to succeed: His Word and prayer. And in the book of Ephesians 4, we are told to put on the whole armor of God. It's a reminder to us to gear up for the battles that we will be facing because 1 John 5:4 (CSB), states, "Everyone who has been born of God conquers the world. This is the victory that has conquered the world: our faith."

---

43 Chris Adams, "3 Lessons for Women's Leaders from Jonah," *Lifeway Women*, 1 Aug. 2011, https://women.lifeway.com/2011/08/01/3-lessons-for-womens-leaders-from-jonah/.
44 Priscilla Shirer, *Life Interrupted: Navigating the Unexpected* (Nashville, TN: B & H Publishing, 2011).

||||||||||||||||||||||||||||||||||||||||||||||||||||||||||||||||||||||||||||||||||

AS CHRISTIANS, WE HAVE BEEN BORN AGAIN, AND IN THIS NEW BIRTH, GOD HAS EQUIPPED US TO BE OVERCOMERS. WE HAVE TO TAKE HOLD OF THAT WHICH HE HAS GIVEN US TO SUCCEED: HIS WORD AND PRAYER.

||||||||||||||||||||||||||||||||||||||||||||||||||||||||||||||||||||||||||||||||||

HARDSHIP QUALIFIES YOU TO OVERCOME

I shared in prior chapters how the suddenness of my mother's death was a life-changing event in my life. At the time, I didn't know that I could live through that hardship. I prayed for my own death and tried to hasten it along by trying to kill myself. I felt that I could not endure the depth of grief I felt, and I wanted a permanent way out because it didn't seem that it was going to end. If you recall, I shared how I took a large knife with me to my bedroom to accomplish what I thought was the only way to get peace.

The Holy Spirit intervened in a supernatural way, and I am not sure exactly what happened because there was no conscious thought on my end to not do it. I went into my bedroom determined. I had had numerous sleepless nights from my SLE and its complications, but also depression kept me awake most nights—but not that night. The only thing I can imagine is that I fell asleep as soon as I got into bed because literally, the next thing I knew, it was the next day. When I awoke, I was stupefied. I had no recollection of going to sleep. If I said I was relieved at that moment that I hadn't completed what I had set out to do, I would be lying.

I wasn't relieved; I woke up still quite depressed and feeling at the end of my rope.

I also, though, as the day progressed, had hope that wasn't there before, and it allowed me to reach out for help. I hadn't been praying after my mom died for several weeks. It was after this attempt that I started to pray again, and I braved going back to church. The book of Jonah is the basis for *Life Interrupted* by Priscilla Shirer. Shirer talks about us running from God. She says:

> *We're running on the inside—running away mentally, running away emotionally, even running away spiritually, painting on a Sunday smile while privately resisting the fellowship God wants, mad that He's doing this to us, mad that we've been blocked and interrupted from the life we really want.*[45]

That summarizes some of what I was feeling during that time of my life and, sometimes, after that time as well. In the next paragraph she states:

> *But in running—even if it's the inside, unseen kind—we place ourselves in the worst possible position we could be in. We stand outside of God's will, outside of His blessing.*[46]

I had a hard time going to church for several reasons, but two of the biggest reasons were that the last place that I saw my mother was in a coffin in the vestibule and at the front of the church. Secondly, it was something my mom and I did together almost every Sunday. It felt that the one place that should offer so much comfort and solace was the one place where I grieved the most, so I avoided the building for several months. When I did go, I would cry as I sat in church, not because of something the pastor

45 Priscilla Shirer, *Life Interrupted: Navigating the Unexpected.*
46 Priscilla Shirer, *Life Interrupted: Navigating the Unexpected.*

said or because of a hymn, but because I was sad and lonely. I just missed my mom.

Tauren Wells's song "God's Not Done With You" is a song that if I were a songwriter, could have been the title track for that season of my life. Some of the lyrics in that song, describing a broken heart, wounds, and scars and feeling lost and falling apart, fit me perfectly. But the rest of the song was true as well: God was not done with me. He did have a plan. He was finishing what He started. And He wasn't done writing my story.[47]

Even now as I am writing, tears are in my eyes as I recall the depth of grief and despair that I felt for so long. I cry now because I still miss my mother, my friend, terribly, but I am so thankful that God was not done with me. Philippians 1:6 says He never quits, and I just have to continue holding on and trusting. As the song "Good Good Father" says: God is perfect in all of His ways. I am loved by Him. And my identity is rooted in His love for me.[48]

In that moment and that stage of my life, being able to recover from my suicide attempt and making the necessary steps to wellness, meant that, finally, I was willing to open my heart, mind, and soul to the love, goodness, and faithfulness of God. I had proven that on my own, I was not able to get over the grief; it was too overwhelming. I had dug a pit, and I was in over my head. Really, the Lord was reaching down, and finally, I grabbed ahold of His hand. (See Psalm 18:16.) I began to trust His Word and His promises, and I chose to stop listening to the lies of the devil.

47 Tauren Wells, vocalist, "God's Not Done With You, written by Tauren Wells, released June 23, 2017, track 10 on *Hills and Valleys*, Provident Label Group.
48 Chris Tomlin, vocalist, "Good Good Father," written by Tony Brown and Pat Barrett, released October 2, 2015, track 1 on *Never Lose Sight*, sixstepsrecords.

It was not easy to go back to church, but in order to regain my sanity and to be able to fully worship God, that was a necessary step. It also showed my ongoing trust and faith in Him. If I was not willing to trust God to do the healing and restoration, then it showed that my faith in Him was lacking. I would not be the overcomer that I am today, and I would not have gotten the victory that I now have, if I didn't allow God to heal my broken heart.

God isn't asking us to fix ourselves. He is asking us to come to Him with all our fears, doubts, brokenness, and heartaches and have faith in Him to do the impossible so that we can be overcomers. Friends, we can never be overcomers if we don't first get over our self-sufficient attitude and learn to first come to Him. I say this to you with all confidence. God will come to you with grace and compassion as undeserved as it truly is. In Psalm 103:4 (HCB), we are reminded that not only will He redeem our lives from the pit, but listen to this: He "crowns you with faithful love and compassion." So, He is waiting on us to come to Him so that we can be overcomers, crowned with love and compassion.

QUALIFICATION IS WORTH THE HURT

As a child of the Most High God, I am now comforted in the truth that He will not waste my pain, and He will not waste your pain. Hardship for each of us looks different but with certain similarities. God knows best and will determine what it looks like, the timing, and what He wants us to learn. In Hebrews 12:11 (NIV), the writer reminds us, "No discipline seems pleasant at the time, but painful. Later on, however, it produces a harvest of righteousness and peace for those who have been trained by it."

In the natural, training implies that we are being prepared for something, and part of the preparation includes repeating certain activities or behaviors until we get them right. So, right away in scripture, we see that the writer of Hebrews is telling us that there will be more than one discipline, more than one hardship, and more than one tribulation. Each hardship should be an opportunity for spiritual growth and maturity. Martin Luther King Jr, in "Letter from Birmingham Jail" on April 16, 1963, said, "The ultimate measure of a man is not where he stands in moments of comfort and convenience, but where he stands at times of challenge and controversy."[49]

According to Hebrews 12, there are two things that we should gain from hardships: righteousness and peace. The biblical concept of peace differs from culture's definition. According to *Baker's Evangelical Dictionary of Biblical Theology*:

> *The biblical concept of peace is larger than that of the worlds and rests heavily on the Hebrew word slm, which means "to be complete" or "to be sound." The verb conveys both a dynamic and a static meaning "to be complete or whole or "to live well."*[50]

We also know that our righteousness is only through Christ. Isaiah 64:6 (NIV) describes our own righteousness as "filthy rags." As we mature in our faith, our righteousness should grow, and a byproduct of that will be peace, according to Isaiah 32:17 (NIV): "The fruit of that righteousness will be peace; its effect will be quietness and confidence forever." If we are immature spiritually, we may not learn what we are supposed to during that time, and God, in His wisdom and providence, may allow other

---

49 Martin Luther King, Jr., "Letter From a Birmingham Jail," *African Studies Center—University of Pennsylvania*, https://www.africa.upenn.edu/Articles_Gen/Letter_Birmingham.html.
50 Walter A. Elwell, *Baker's Dictionary of Theology* (Grand Rapids, MI: Baker Book House, 1996).

circumstances in our lives so that we can become mature in our faith and accomplish His purpose.

James, the brother of Jesus, tells us that we should do the following:

Consider it pure joy, my brothers and sisters, whenever you face trials of many kinds, because you know that the testing of your faith produces perseverance. Let perseverance finish its work so that you may be mature and complete, not lacking anything.
—James 1:2-4 (NIV)

In these scriptures, we see that hardships may be a testing of our faith, and as we persevere, we will be rewarded—although maybe not in the way we expect to be rewarded. The reward here is that we will be spiritually mature and complete. In Romans 8:29, we are told that as disciples of Christ, part of the maturity process here on earth is that we are predestined to be conformed to the image of Jesus Christ. Obviously, this is not an easy task, and it is only accomplished through the finished work of the cross and the present working of the Holy Spirit living in and through us as we live yielded lives.

God does work in mysterious ways; He sprinkles His blessings in order to make the task of overcoming a bit easier. He does this by giving us healing in the midst of a hardship. Shortly after healing a bit from my bowel surgery, getting used to the colostomy bag, and preparing to start my new job, I took my first European trip to Rome, Italy. It was already planned—like a last hurrah after finishing the movement disorder fellowship. I planned to attend a neurological conference, and I didn't want to miss it. It was a great trip.

After I got back, I started my new job. My colostomy bag was to be in for a total of six months because my surgeon and the other doctors were concerned about all my other health issues at the time. I suffered two bouts of small bowel obstruction and had to be hospitalized. During the second hospitalization, the surgeon realized surgery was needed to correct the obstruction and decided to just go ahead and remove the colostomy bag. Say, hallelujah! I went through two extra hospitalizations, a few days at Rockdale Medical Center, a few more days at Northside Hospital, and then several days of excruciating pain from the small bowel obstruction, but I can see the silver lining now. I didn't see the silver lining at all at the time. In fact, it was so bad at times I prayed for death, but the result was that the colostomy was taken out three months early.

During the first few days of being back home after having the colostomy bag removed, I suffered a setback. I remember sitting on the sofa and getting a whiff of something horrible. I couldn't believe that it was me until I stood up and realized that my bandages were soaked. I touched and smelled it and knew right away that it was probably infected. My mother and grandmother were still alive, so we called the surgeon, and he said come to the office the next day. We did, and he had to undo the lower half of my very long incision. He used blue cloths that looked like kitchen towels to soak up the purulent material coming out of the wound. I was shocked. At that point in my medical career, I had never seen that much puss-filled material come from a recent surgical wound. He had to leave it open to heal, and that took six months.

I remember my grandmother coming to stay with me for a few months because my mother had to go back to NYC for work. I will never forget my grandmother's face when she first had to help me pack that hole. It was awe and disbelief. She had tears in her eyes. I saw it and felt it and related to it because that had also been my reaction when I first saw it. For several weeks, we had to pack the hole with gauzes—not gauze, but gauzes soaked in vinegar and water. It was amazing to be doing this because after several weeks, I noticed that I was using less and less gauze.

On the surface, it didn't seem like it was healing because I still had an open wound that was not pretty to look at day after day. My life felt like one prolonged attack with no respite, and at times, I would doubt God's presence and protection. When we doubt His protection, we can go back to Scripture. Jesus, in John 10:11 (NIV), states, "I am the good shepherd. The good shepherd lays down his life for the sheep." In *At the Table with Jesus*, Louie Giglio describes how Jesus does that:

> *The shepherd was the gate, which is exactly what Jesus communicated to His disciples. Jesus is the door through which we enter God's kingdom. He is the gate. And when we are part of His flock, there is nothing that can reach us or harm us or even touch us without going through Him. Therefore, we can come in and go out and find pasture.*[51]

It is simply amazing that through the trials, He is with us, and He continues to be our Good Shepherd, sticking to His promises because He is faithful. He never leaves us or forsakes us, and we don't need to be afraid or discouraged.

51 Louie Giglio, *At the Table with Jesus: 66 Days to Draw Closer to Christ and Fortify Your Faith* (Nashville, TN: Thomas Nelson, 2022).

THERE'S A METHOD TO QUALIFICATION

As overcomers, we know that we don't need to be afraid or discouraged as we encounter battles, but it comes with training and knowing that ultimately all the battles that we face belong to the Lord. (See 2 Chronicles 20:21-22.) We need to be reminded of this fact daily and have the right gear, listed below and detailed in Ephesians 6:11-13:

1) Belt of Truth
2) Breastplate of Righteousness
3) Sandals of Peace
4) Shield of Faith
5) Helmet of Salvation
6) Sword of the Spirit (Bible)

I am sure it hasn't missed your attention that included in our armor are two of the things that we learned and read about in Hebrews 12 that are a byproduct of God's discipline: righteousness and peace.

In a chapter on hardships, it is paramount that I discuss God's armor, what it means, and why we need to wear it. Literally, we are going to need to put on God's armor daily.

According to historical writings, the armor of a Roman soldier weighed about seventy pounds. It's not hard to imagine how vital the apostle Paul said it was to stand against the enemy:

Stand, therefore with TRUTH like a BELT around your waist, RIGHTEOUSNESS like ARMOR on your chest, and your feet SANDALED with READINESS FOR THE GOSPEL of PEACE. In every situation take up the SHIELD of FAITH with which you can extinguish all the flaming arrows of the evil one. Take the HELMET of SALVATION and SWORD

*of the Spirit which is the WORD of GOD. PRAY at all times
in the Spirit with every prayer and request and stay alert with
all perseverance and intercession for all the saints. —Ephesians
6:14-18 (CSB, emphasis added)*

I included verse 18 because after listening to a sermon by
Priscilla Shirer. She made the point that PRAYER should be
part of the whole armor. It is not normally included, but her
argument is profound. In doing research, I read an article written
by Bill Mounce titled "Is Prayer Part of God's Armor?" In this
article, he concludes:

*Every part of our armor must be donned with prayer and alert-
ness—all prayers and petitions, uttered at all times, with all
perseverance and petition for all the saints. . . . Prayer wraps
itself around all of our spiritual armor and enables us to stand
against Satan and his evil forces.*[52]

It wasn't just my prayers but the prayers of my mother, grandmother, aunts, and other friends and family that kept me through
some of the darkest moments of my life. We live in a sin-cursed
world, and that means that we will have trials and tribulations,
but the Bible cautions us to put on righteousness as part of
God's armor. Priscilla Shirer, in her sermon "The Armor," calls
righteousness "right side up living that invites God's favor and
his blessings on our lives."[53] Unrighteousness is upside-down
behavior, choosing not to live in alignment with God's Word,
and that creates an environment that invites the enemy to come
and make himself at home in my life. As we put on righteousness,

---

52 Bill Mounce, "Is Prayer Part of God's Armor? (Eph 6:18)," *Bill Mounce*, 8 Aug. 2021. https://www.
billmounce.com/monday-with-mounce/prayer-part-gods-armor-eph-6-18#:~:text=Every%20part%20
of%20our%20armor,petition%2C%20for%20all%20the%20saints.
53 Going Beyond Ministries with Priscilla Shirer, "The Armor," 46:54, 31 Aug. 2017, https://youtu.be/
ePbAv6NuKzQ.

we are choosing to live our lives in alignment with the Word of God—not perfection, but girded by the truth of God's Word.

||||||||||||||||||||||||||||||||||||||||||||||||||||||||||||||||||||||||||||||||||||||||

AS WE PUT ON RIGHTEOUSNESS, WE ARE CHOOSING TO LIVE OUR LIVES IN ALIGNMENT WITH THE WORD OF GOD—NOT PERFECTION, BUT GIRDED BY THE TRUTH OF GOD'S WORD.

||||||||||||||||||||||||||||||||||||||||||||||||||||||||||||||||||||||||||||||||||||||||

We are to affirm God's standard by making sure that how we behave and how we live our lives are congruent with the truth of God. It means that if we live unrighteous lives, we are outside the will of God, and we are giving the devil a "foothold." We may keep praying, but instead of answered prayers, we'll notice that the enemy is still running rampant in our lives. It may, in part, rest on the fact that we are not living lives that glorify God. We have to then examine ourselves and ask the Holy Spirit to correct any upside-down living in our lives because we cannot do it on our own. (See 2 Corinthians 13:5.)

Most of the weight of a Roman soldier's armor was in the breastplate, and the belt helped to distribute the weight. So, it is also spiritually that Jesus—the Truth—found in John 14:6," I am the way, the truth and the life," will help us correct the upside-down living. When we accepted Christ as Lord of our lives, the righteousness of God was deposited in us. (See 2

Corinthians 5:21 and Romans 5:9.) We now must put it on and walk it out daily when we gear up for battle.

IF IT QUALIFIED THEM, IT WILL QUALIFY YOU

I love to read about the different battles in the Old Testament—at times too bloody, but there is a wealth of information about faith and utter dependence on God in them. One of my favorites tells the story of King Jehoshaphat of Judah and three enemies who decided to team up against him. The Moabites, Ammonites, and Meunites, according to scripture were a vast number. Jehoshaphat and all his people were afraid. Like the true ruler that he was, the first thing first he acknowledged was that fear, and the Bible describes what he did with it: "He resolved to seek the Lord. Then he proclaimed a fast for all Judah" (2 Chronicles 20:3, CSB). Next, he led a corporate prayer—one of the most powerful prayers recorded in the Bible.

It was bold and beautiful!:

Lord, God of our ancestors, are you not the God who is in heaven, and to you not rule over all the kingdoms of the nations? Power and might are in your hand and no one can stand against you. Are you not our God who drove out the inhabitants of this land before your people Israel and who gave it forever to the descendants of Abraham your friend? They have lived in the land and have built you a sanctuary in it for your name and have said, "If disaster comes on us—sword or judgment, pestilence or famine— we will stand before this temple and before you, for your name is in the temple. We will cry out to you because of our distress, and you will hear and deliver."

Now here are the Ammonites, Moabites and the inhabitants of Mount Seir. You did not let Israel invade them when Israel came out of the land of Egypt, but Israel turned away from them and did not destroy them. Look how they repay us coming to drive us out of your possession that you gave us as an inheritance. Our God, will you not judge them? For we are powerless before this vast number that comes to fight against us. We do not know what to do but we look to you. —2 Chronicles 3:6-12 (CSB)

I love this scripture! The LORD's response is even more powerful! "Do not be afraid or discouraged because of the vast number, for the battle is not yours, but God's" (2 Chronicles 3:13, CSB).

Cue in Yolanda Adam's song "The Battle Is the Lord's." She eloquently sings the words, reminding us that Jesus feels our pain, sadness, and sorrow and heals our hurts. Whatever we are going through God is using it for His glory. We just need to hold our heads up, stick our chests out, and remember that the battle is not ours. It's the Lord's![54]

Further in the passage, God continues to speak:

"You do not have to fight this battle. Position yourselves, stand still, and see the salvation of the Lord. He is with you, Judah and Jerusalem. Do not be afraid or discouraged. Tomorrow, go out to face them, for the Lord is with you." —2 Chronicles 3:17 (CSB)

Our God knows that, sometimes, we need to hear certain things more than once. He recognized their fear and didn't chastise them for it but reiterated to them that it was not necessary. In today's vernacular, we would say, "God's got this," and we need a daily or maybe hourly reminder of this fact. We don't have to

---

54 Yolanda Adams, vocalist, "The Battle Is the Lord's," by V. Michael McKay, released October 19, 1993, track 2 on *Save the World*, Verity Records.

fight, but we must show up. How we show up matters; we can't come to battle our adversaries whining, doubtful, fearful, or discouraged. King Jehoshaphat and his people show us how we ought to show up daily:

As they were about to go out, Jehoshaphat stood and said, "Hear me, Judah and you inhabitants of Jerusalem. Believe in the Lord your God, and you will be established; believe in his prophets, and you will succeed." Then he consulted with the people and appointed some to sing for the Lord and some to praise the splendor of his holiness. When they went out in front of the armed forces, they kept singing:

Give thanks to the Lord,
for his faithful love endures forever.

THE MOMENT they began their shouts and praises, the Lord set an ambush against the Ammonites, Moabites, and the inhabitants of Mount Seir who came to fight against Judah, and they were defeated. The Ammonites and Moabites turned against the inhabitants of Mount Seir and COMPLETELY ANNIHILATED THEM. When they had finished with the inhabitants of Seir, they helped destroy each other. —2 Chronicles 3:20-23 (CSB, emphasis added)

If you were not familiar with this battle and just read it for the first time, you can easily see why I get so excited about it. We, personally, don't have literal armies against us, but we sure have an adversary in the form of the devil, and we have battles that we face each day. It may feel like life is ganging up on you as I felt at different seasons of my life like it was doing. So, whether it is one hardship or several, the Lord is saying the same thing to me and to you today. I believe it would be something like this: "Marsha, put on the armor of God, position yourself, stand still (not *passive* as it may seem by standard definition), and watch Me win this for you so that I get the glory from your life!"

In 2018, Pastor Eric preached a sermon titled "You stay here. I'm going up!" He preached about how we must encourage ourselves as we go through hardships and trials. He kept repeating, "God Himself." The phrase "God Himself" allows us to keep climbing, keep stepping out in faith because there are some things only God can fix. It was preached even before I moved to Cincinnati, but I enjoy listening to sermons, and how appropriate it is that I listed to that sermon as I wrote this book! "God Himself" is a great reminder for our hearts and minds. We know the track record of our God. We can look back at His faithfulness and know that through any hardships, God is with us. Yes—God Himself!

The worshipers knew the track record of God and that God Himself would provide the victory that they needed. It wouldn't come from their warriors but from God Himself. Worshipers were placed ahead of the army, and if you read the entire chapter, you will read a portion where Jehoshaphat asked the people to have faith not just in God but also in the prophets so that they could be successful.

I thought that it was odd for him to tell them to have faith in the prophets until the Holy Spirit made it clear to me. We must have faith in God to win battles, but sometimes, God will place others in our lives to help us succeed: our pastor, Godly family members and friends, and, of course, the local church body. We do need to be in tune with the Holy Spirit to be able to discern His voice for guidance and to know whose voice to listen to. But as we grow in our faith and our spiritual relationship, it will become clearer and easier each time.

YOUR PAIN IS SOMEONE ELSE'S GAIN

As we remember the great stories of the Old Testament and ponder the whole Armor of God, we are encouraged that during hardship, we have to make a decision on how to react to ensure that we remain faithful in our trust and confidence in God. I have come to realize that trials and hardships are not always about what *we* are meant to learn, but, as God gets the glory, others are looking at us, and they are also learning. People we love and even people we don't have a close relationship with are watching to see what makes us different as followers of Christ. While they are doing this every day, they do it especially during visible hardships.

We have often heard the following: "Values are caught— not taught." "Character is not taught; it is caught." "Wisdom is caught, not taught." And I love the Scottish version: "Some things are better felt than telt." So, as we go through hardship, a key point to always remember is that our family, friends, and coworkers are looking on, and our hardships may be for them as much as for us.

Viktor Frankl states this in *Man's Search for Meaning*:

We who have lived in concentration camps can remember the men who walked through the huts comforting others, giving away their last piece of bread. They may have been few in number, but they offer sufficient proof that everything can be taken from a man but one thing: the last of the human freedoms—to choose one's attitude in any given set of circumstances, to choose one's own way.[55]

When I read Elie Wiesel's Nobel Peace Prize-winning book, *Night*, several years ago and in this autobiography, he recounted his survival as a teenager in the Nazi death camps. Several quotes stood out, and I will mention one here because it fits as we go through hardships now in the twenty-first century:

No one is as capable of gratitude as one who has emerged from the kingdom of night. We know that every moment is a moment of grace, every hour an offering; not to share them would mean to betray them. Our lives no longer belong to us alone; they belong to all those who need us desperately.[56]

Jesus tells us that we ought to "Love the Lord your God with all your heart, with all your soul and with all your mind. This is the greatest and most important command. The second is like it: Love your neighbor as yourself. All the Law and the Prophets depend on these two commands." In the Biblical sense our neighbor is not relegated just to the geographical sense but instead includes those that may not look, act or think like us. It may also include someone we have just met in passing. It includes family and friends.

I challenge myself and I challenge you to think that one way we can show love to our neighbors is to suffer well. Hebrews 12:15 (CSB) says, "Make sure that no one falls short of the grace of God and that no root of bitterness springs up, causing trouble and defiling many." Let us go through our sufferings in such a way that the words we say, the things we do, and even our every attitude

---

55 Viktor E. Frankl, Harold S. Kushner, and William J. Winslade, *Man's Search for Meaning*, (Boston, MA: Beacon Press, 2006).
56 Elie Wiesel, *Night* (New York, NY: Spark Publishing, 2014).

reveal that God is real, He is love, He cares, and His grace is more than enough to see us through. Love, be grateful, be thankful, and comfort others because according to the apostle Paul:

Blessed be the God and Father of our Lord Jesus Christ, the Father of mercies and the God of all comfort. He comforts us in all our affliction, so that we may be able to comfort those who are in any kind of affliction, through the comfort we ourselves receive from God. For just as the sufferings of Christ overflow to us, so also through Christ our comfort overflows. —2 Corinthians 1:3-4 (CSB)

WE ARE NOT A ONE-MAN ARMY

In chapter 4, I wrote about the three Hebrew boys from Daniel 3 and how they were thrown into a furnace of blazing fire. Beth Moore, in her Bible study of the book of Daniel, teaches about three possible outcomes when the people of God face a fiery trial.

1) We can be delivered from the fire. The benefit of this outcome is that our faith is built.
2) We can be delivered through the fire. The benefit here is that our faith is refined.
3) We can be delivered by the fire straight into God's arms. In this case, our faith is perfected.[57]

She also makes a statement that we can be emboldened by:

Each man was flanked by the power and presence of God the Father, Son and Holy Spirit. In heavenly mathematics, the sum total of those in the fire is always four: one believer plus a holy Trinity.[58]

---

57 Beth Moore, *Daniel: Lives of Integrity, Words of Prophecy* (Nashville, TN: LifeWay Press, 2011).
58 Beth Moore, *Daniel: Lives of Integrity.*

And we are encouraged because the statement reminds us that we are never alone. The company that is with us is divine and all-powerful. In Isaiah 43:2, God reminds us that we may pass through the waters and walk through the fire, but we will not be overwhelmed, and we will not be scorched because of the Lord our God and Savior.

At Citygate Church, we often sing a song written by Elyssa Smith and performed by Michael W. Smith. It's called "Surrounded (Fight My Battles)." There is a part that repeats, "It may look like I'm surrounded, but I'm surrounded by You."[59] That is how we fight our battles, and I am reminded of this song when I read about another battle in 2 Kings. I first read this story when I lived in Atlanta and was teaching Sunday school at Heritage Hills Baptist Church. Elisha was with his servant, and the king of Aram was upset with Elisha because he was helping the king of Israel. Elisha's servant was very nervous. When he awoke and went outside, Elisha's servant saw that they were surrounded by an army. The conversation went like this:

"Oh, my master, what are we to do?"

Elisha said, "Don't be afraid, for those who are with us outnumber those who are with them."

Then Elisha prayed, "Lord, please open his eyes and let him see." So the Lord opened the servant's eyes, and he saw that the mountain was covered with horses and chariots of fire all around Elisha. —2 Kings 6:15-17 (CSB)

---

59 Michael W. Smith, vocalist, "Surrounded (Fight My Battles)," by Elyssa Smith, released February 23, 2018, track 8 on *Surrounded*, Rocketown.

Elisha prayed that God would open the eyes of his servant to see that the enemies were surrounded by the army of the Living God. And the Lord did.

Pastor Tony Evans's Study Bible includes sections he calls "HOPE WORDS." Near 2 Kings, he writes the following Hope Words, "You get sight in the spiritual realm when you exercise faith in the physical realm."[60] So, as we go through our daily struggles—maybe yearly struggles for some of us—we must live in the physical realm, but our hope lies in the spiritual realm. It matters not what it looks like; we can keep praising and believing that we will see the victory.

As we walk through the valleys, we are utilizing faith, trusting in the unknown because we know who holds our tomorrow. My grandmother used to sing this song quite a lot, and my mom and I would also sing it: "I Know Who Holds Tomorrow." Ira F. Stanphill, a mid-twentieth-century songwriter, wrote, "Many things about tomorrow I don't seem to understand, but I know who holds tomorrow, and I know who holds my hand."[61]

|||||||||||||||||||||||||||||||||||||||||||||||||||||||||||||||||||||||||||||||||||||||||||||||||||||

AS WE WALK THROUGH THE VALLEYS, WE ARE UTILIZING FAITH, TRUSTING IN THE UNKNOWN BECAUSE WE KNOW WHO HOLDS OUR TOMORROW.

|||||||||||||||||||||||||||||||||||||||||||||||||||||||||||||||||||||||||||||||||||||||||||||||||||||

60 *The Tony Evans Study Bible: Advancing God's Kingdom Agenda* (Nashville, TN: Holman Bibles, 2019).
61 Ira F. Stanphill, "I Know Who Holds Tomorrow" (Brentwood, TN: Singspiration Music, copyright renewed 1978).

The 2 Kings story gives us a glimpse of God's provision and presence. It is a daily reminder that we are never alone. No matter the battle we face, the Lord's army is on our side. We have the indwelling of His Spirit active and living within us, giving us the strength to be overcomers because unseen battles are continually being fought on our behalf in the heavenly realm.

In the book of Daniel, we also get a glimpse of and are reminded that war is being fought daily on our behalf by unseen forces. In Daniel 10, Daniel had a vision and was told something quite fascinating. Daniel had been in mourning and had fasted for twenty-one days but got no response from God during that time. An angel showed up on day twenty-four and spoke:

He said to me, "Daniel, you are a man who is highly precious. . . .

"Do not be afraid . . . for from the first day that you pur-posed to understand and to humble yourself before your God, your words were heard, and I have come in response to them. However, the prince of the kingdom of Persia opposed me for twenty-one days. Then Michael, one of the chief princes, came to help me, for I had been left there with the kings of Persia."
—Daniel 10:11–13 (BSB)

We are never given insight into Daniel's thoughts during the twenty-one days that he was mourning and fasting. If he was like us, when we are going through dark times, our minds start to wander, and we doubt. During times of hardship, when I pray, I want God to intervene immediately, to be my own "genie in a bottle." When, day after day or month after month, nothing changes, I start to doubt His love and care for me. God's timing and ours are not the same. (See 2 Peter 3:8.) So, we hold on tight to God during these times, and we trust His heart, especially when we can't see Him clearly at work. Psalm 68:19 reminds us that the Lord daily bears our burdens, and that brings me comfort.

FAITHFUL DILIGENCE IN MIND, HEART, AND ACTION

I had to learn to put God first and to make spending time in His presence a priority. I had to figure out what making God a priority looks like—practically. It means going to Him first thing in the morning. It is going to Him first when I am faced with difficulties—before I call someone to lament about it. It means, like Paul says in 1 Thessalonians 5, that I pray without ceasing. Therefore, throughout my day, I am seeking His counsel or just telling Him thanks or other things about my day. Lastly, I meet with Him at the end of the day. I don't always get it right, but I keep striving, and the more I spend time in His presence, the easier it gets.

There was a song we sang when I was growing up in Jamaica. It was called "I Keep Falling in Love with Him." The lyrics describe how we fall in love with the Lord over and over every day and how that love gets sweeter and sweeter as the days go by.[62] Then, in Psalm 34:8 (NIV), David invites us to "taste and see that the Lord is good." He says we are blessed if we take refuge in Him. So let's be reminded to take refuge in our God and to remember: "The eternal God is your refuge, and underneath are the everlasting arms" (Deuteronomy 33:27, NIV). Over and over in the Scriptures, we read that God is our refuge, and that gives us strength because we realize that we can seek refuge in Him and know that God will fight our battles.

---

62 The Lanny Wolfe Trio, vocalists, "I Keep Falling in Love With Him," by Lanny Wolfe, released 1997, track 3 on *An Evening With the Lanny Wolfe Trio*, Impact Records.

As you read, you may have realized how much scriptures and songs have helped me along my journey. It's no coincidence because in singing, we are worshiping, and when we worship, we are inviting the presence of the Lord into our lives.

Psalm 23 is a well-known and beloved passage of scripture. In verse 5, David talks about God preparing a table for us in the presence of our enemies. I believe this has several meanings, and the one that the Holy Spirit has illuminated at different times in my life and that brings comfort to my soul isn't so much that my enemies are seeing me prosper. For me, it's an image that I may be surrounded by enemies, trials, and hardships, but in spite of all that is going on around me, God has a bounty that He has prepared. We can still partake even as we are going through by faith. Blessings will continue to flow, God's favor will still be on our lives, and it will be evident to those around us if we continue to walk by faith as we stand, praise, pray, and trust through the trials.

As I have written about life's hardships, I can also talk about God's blessings. He has blessed me more than I could have asked or imagined, and He has allowed me to live as He has promised. He came that we may have abundant life. Abundance and blessings, we often think, come monetarily. Even though those are blessings that He wants us to have, it is so much more than that if we would just seek His kingdom and His righteousness.

David, God states, was a man after His own heart. That really gives me hope because David questioned God, he got upset with God, he praised God, and he left us with some of the most quoted scriptures in the book of Psalms. When I struggle with depression, Psalm 16:11 (LSB) brings me peace: "You will make known to me the path of life; In Your presence is fullness of joy;

In Your right hand there are pleasures forever." In Sunday school as a child, I sang, "In His presence there is fullness of joy. At His right-hand pleasures for evermore. Oh, what fellowship divine! I am His, and He is mine. In the presence of the Lord, there's fullness of joy." And He has put eternity in our hearts, according to Ecclesiastes 3:11 (CSB), "He has made everything appropriate in its time. He has also put eternity in their hearts, but no one can discover the work God has done from beginning to end."

I have made it through over twenty years of SLE and its myriad of complications, and by God's grace and mercy, I completed medical school, neurology residency, and fellowship training. I am now working full-time in private practice and affiliated with several hospitals. I have had moments throughout all these years when I felt like I was literally in survival mode, not really living— just surviving instead of thriving. If you are currently just hanging in there, I would like to say to you, "Don't give up! Keep believing what God said to you from the very beginning!"

I remember so often getting frustrated and being doubtful, but each time I had to go back to the character of God, what I knew to be true of God. I prayed, and the very opposite of what I prayed for would happen: "Father, I pray that I will have a day free of pain." And after having prayed that, I had some of the worse pain days! I would wonder to myself, *Why did I even pray today?* I would get anxious about how the day was going to go once the pain started. Would it affect my walking, my breathing? On those days, I still went to school, or I went about seeing patients and being the best doctor I could be for them that day.

I am sure there were days that I was grouchy and not my best self. However, I often surprised myself that I was able to make it through the day without crying, giving up, or leaving early, not knowing how or why, and sometimes asking myself, *What happened here?* I had some days when my depression was so tangible that it took all I had to get up, go, and not cry in front of patients or their families. On some of the days that I felt at my worse physically and emotionally, patients would leave a positive review about how I helped them. Can I tell you that at the end of the day—or maybe not that day but a couple days later—I would look back and say, "God, it was only You, and I thank You!" "Thank You for Your strength," and I continued to believe and would state that by *His stripes,* I am healed.

I learned to walk in the statement of healing, not giving up, not staying home and wallowing in self-pity, and not going on disability but walking in what I believed and what God promised. If I am healed, that means I could go out to work and accomplish God's will and purpose for my life. I was blessed to have a God-fearing grandmother and mother who talked to God regularly on my behalf, so I could trust them to give Godly wisdom and advice. You may very well get frustrated like I did and still struggle, but once you are sure you have heard from God, do not doubt, especially when time seems to be running out, and nothing has changed. When it seems like the very opposite of what you have prayed for has happened, stay strong!

I got impatient at times because in my head, it was taking too long for me to see the reality of my healing, but then I would be reminded of King David. Immediately after he was *anointed* to be king, we see him going back to being a shepherd instead of being taken to the palace. (See 1 Samuel 16.) However, we are also told that the Spirit of the Lord came powerfully on David from that day forward. So, he had the promise of a kingship but not yet the crown. He had a down payment of the promise in the form of the Spirit of the Lord. Can you relate? I know I can. As we wait, we can trust the Spirit of the Lord that we have been sealed with, according to Ephesians 1:13 (CSB): "In him you also were sealed with the promised Holy Spirit when you heard the word of truth, the gospel of your salvation, and when you believed."

Pastor Dharius Daniels, in a recent sermon, asked what we do when our oil and our season don't match. He calls it the *God Gap*—God intentionally orchestrates it so that He can use the distance as development of the back side of the blessing. Friends, don't rush the timing because God is using the gaps (the time spent waiting on our promise/our healing) to grow and mature us for His service and for our good.

So, to sum it all up, this is what I have learned throughout the years, and I continue to learn:

» Walk in what God has told you, do not waver, and do not turn to the right or to the left.

» To find solace and victory, memorize scriptures. Be grounded in truth because Hebrews 4:12 (NIV) says that "the word of God is alive and active." I know it may sound stressful, and you are probably already saying, "I can't memorize scriptures!" Why do I know that you are saying that? Well, because I have said it many a time. However, I have realized the beauty of the Holy Spirit in many things, and one thing is that even if I don't verbatim remember the scripture, or even exactly where in the Bible it is found, I can still benefit from knowing some or most of the words because, without a doubt, the Holy Spirit will intervene!

» It is better to know the scriptures before the trials begin because when we are deep in our trials, we may not be able to read the Bible in a given moment. We may not have the strength—and in some cases, we may not have the desire—to read the Bible. However, if you already have scriptures memorized, they will readily come to mind with the help of the Holy Spirit because our mind already has a trench that has been made by our continual pursuit of His Word. If you are currently in the midst of the trial, and you don't have any scripture memorized, I encourage you to get an audible version of the Bible.

» Listen to sermons, not just on Sundays but multiple times throughout the week so that you can saturate your eyes and ears with God's Word. That will minimize the ability of the devil to get a foothold.

» Finally, as you go through, don't forget to WORSHIP because it will always usher us into God's presence. (See Psalm 22:3.) In another chapter, I wrote about the manifest presence of God, and that is what we should all long for, actually crave it as we do our next breath. Worship will allow us to experience His shekinah glory!

Be encouraged by Beth Moore:

Our God is able to deliver us, Beloved. Every time! And how often He does! If ever He does not and the flames of death or tragedy consume us, it is to light a fire somewhere and in some heart that can never be extinguished. Trust Him to the death. Trust Him through the death. In the blink of an eye, we'll understand.

God will choose how and when He will deliver. One thing we can and must do is trust Him through the process. We are only overcomers when we trust in Him—Jesus Christ, our Lord and Savior!

CHAPTER 6

Lessons in Grief and Pain (Nothing Is Wasted)

"He heals the brokenhearted and binds up their wounds."
—Psalm 147:3 (NIV)

The *Collins English Dictionary* defines grief as "a feeling of extreme sadness" and "acute sorrow."[63] Synonyms that may mean more for others are agony, anguish, distress, torment, brokenhearted, lamentation, bereavement, and despondency.[64] These are just a few of the options. It is associated with the death of a loved one as well as loss of any kind: marriage via divorce, close friendship, job, and even a dream.

GRIEF COMES IN STAGES

In 1969, Dr. Elisabeth Kübler-Ross authored a book on death titled *On Death and Dying: What the Dying Have to Teach Doctors, Nurses, Clergy and Their Own Families.* In it, she first outlined the now-famous five stages of death: denial, anger, bargaining, depression, and acceptance.[65] In another transformative book, co-authored with David Kessler just prior to her death in 2004, *On Grief and Grieving: Finding the Meaning of Grief Through the Five Stages of Loss,* she and Kessler adapted the stages introduced previously in *On Death and Dying* to the much-needed area of grief.[66]

Since then, David Kessler has commented that the five stages "were never meant to help tuck messy emotions into neat packages. They are responses to loss that many people have, but there is not a typical response to loss as there is no typical loss."[67] Ideally these stages were meant to be used as a framework to help us

---

63 "Grief Definition and Meaning," *Collins English Dictionary,* https://www.collinsdictionary.com/us/dictionary/english/grief.
64 "Synonyms of Grief," *Thesaurus.com,* https://www.thesaurus.com/browse/grief.
65 Elisabeth Kübler-Ross, On Death and Dying: What the Dying Have to Teach Doctors, Nurses, Clergy and Their Own Families (New York, NY: Quality Paperback Book Club, 2002).
66 Elisabeth Kübler-Ross and David Kessler, *On Grief and Grieving: Finding the Meaning of Grief through the Five Stages of Loss* (New York , NY: Scribner, 2014).
67 David Kessler, "Five Stages of Grief by Elisabeth Kubler Ross & David Kessler," *Grief.com,* https://grief.com/the-five-stages-of-grief/.

identify our feelings as we navigate the terrain of grief and make us better equipped to cope with life after the loss.

I will briefly review the five stages of grief and what they mean as per the Grief.com website:

» Denial helps us to survive the loss, but also during this stage, the world becomes meaningless and overwhelming. We are in a state of shock, we feel numb, and we're not sure how we can go on or if we can go on. "There is grace in denial."

» Anger comes next. We are encouraged to feel it and embrace it because as we do that, it will fade away more quickly. Anger can feel like "strength, and it can be an anchor, giving temporary structure to the nothingness of loss."

» Bargaining leads to struggling to find meaning, and we may become lost in the maze of "What if" and "If only" statements.

» Depression then tends to set in, during which we may feel overwhelmed and helpless. Here, grief tends to go to a much deeper level, and it may feel as if it will never get better, but it is worthwhile to point out that it is an appropriate response. Depression, however, can become a part of complicated grief or grief-related major depression, and it can become chronic, lead to self-harm or ideation, become disabling, and affect a person's quality of life.

» Acceptance comes as we are now able to accept the reality of the loss and recognize that there is a new reality—the permanent reality without our loved one being a part of it. At times, others may think that when we get to this stage, we are okay, but for those grieving, it may simply be that they are experiencing more good than bad days. Acceptance may occur in stages. As we let go of the past, it may first be in bits and pieces at a time; then we start to reach forward, forging new connections, new relationships, and new dreams.[68]

I would also add that the stages aren't linear. We may spend different amounts of time in each stage and may cycle back and forth from one stage to another. The crucial thing about grief is that it must be dealt with, and real life cannot start again until it is. If it's not, we are just existing. I have had to learn to live in what I call the "new normal." It's a normal that still honors, trusts, and acknowledges that God is a good, good Father. I can still miss my mother and be thankful for the time that I had her as my mother.

THE CRUCIAL THING ABOUT GRIEF IS THAT IT MUST BE DEALT WITH, AND REAL LIFE CANNOT START AGAIN UNTIL IT IS.

Recently, David Kessler introduced a sixth stage in his new book titled *Finding Meaning: The Sixth Stage of Grief.* He writes, "Meaning is a reflection of the love we have for those we have lost. Meaning is the sixth stage of grief, the stage where the healing often resides."[69] At first glance, it seems odd that finding meaning would be a stage of grief, but it is, and I will try my best to explain what the author means.

68 David Kessler, "Five Stages of Grief . . . " *Grief.com*, https://grief.com/the-five-stages-of-grief/.
69 David Kessler, *Finding Meaning: The Sixth Stage of Grief* (New York, NY: Scribner, 2020).

As he has counseled people through loss, Kessler has found that "the person who sees death as sacred has found a way to find meaning *in it*. To those who get mired in a seemingly endless slog of grief, death feels utterly devoid of meaning."[70] He goes on to give insight into how we can remember, in a healthy way, those who have died. Healthy grief includes grieving with more love and less pain. It shows us how we can move on with our lives by living in a way that honors our loved ones. And, Kessler says it's up to us:

> *It is in your control to find meaning every day. You can still love, laugh, grow, pray, smile cry, live, give, be grateful, be present. You can take the other moments as they come. That can be the meaning. In the end, no matter how hard it is, if we allow ourselves to spend time searching for the meaning in our loss, it will appear because of our search and the healing will happen. . . . Wherever you find it, meaning matters and meaning heals.*[71]

As Christians, we know that we find the meaning through our belief and trust in God and as we allow the Holy Spirit to heal our broken hearts.

TAKE THE STAGE AND GRIEVE

I told you my mother's death was sudden, totally unexpected, and life-changing. I went through most of the stages listed above. Often, they overlapped. During the first few months and years after her death, as I tried to move forward with my life, I realized it was never going to be the same. Life, the way I knew it, had

---

70 David Kessler, *Finding Meaning: The Sixth Stage of Grief.*
71 David Kessler, *Finding Meaning: The Sixth Stage of Grief.*

ceased to exist. I had to start imagining how my new life—my new normal—would look.

I described earlier what it was like as I walked into the emergency room at Southern Ohio Medical Center and approached Room 1: the medical staff, EKG leads on her chest, portable ultrasound, people talking at the same time. . . . Most clear, though, is that I heard, "Call it," and another voice declared the time of death: 11:10 a.m. The staff outside the room knew who I was and that I was waiting just outside. The inside staff hadn't recognized that I was there until after they had declared the time of death and turned around.

I was in such a state of denial and anger that it was hard to think straight, but the staff allowed me to go to her, sit beside her, put my head on her chest, and kiss her cheeks for what I thought was the last time. But I was wrong; I was able to give one last kiss on the day of her funeral service. When we meet in heaven, what a rejoicing that will be for the great family reunion!

I remember the staff and my office manager asking if I needed to call someone. At the time, I wasn't sure where my phone was, and I could hardly remember the phone numbers for my aunts in Jamaica. I called my mother's best friend and eventually was able to speak to my aunts and give them the news. I am forever thankful for my immediate family who came up from Jamaica that same night. It meant I wasn't alone on that first night. I'm thankful also for my manager at the time and other coworkers who all chipped in in so many tangible ways, and as a result, we were able to bury my mother in one week. Dr. Rosenberg's wife, right away, went out with some instructions from me and found the perfect resting place, shaded and under a tree.

While I was no longer in denial, per se, as stated, some of my grief stages were overlapping. Anger, depression, and isolation fought for my emotions for quite some time. My anger was tri-fold: directed at myself, God, and my mother. I was upset with myself because I was the one who took the job in Portsmouth. I bought the house even though we both thought the driveway was difficult to navigate. I blamed God because He could have stopped it all, and He did not. I was upset with Him because He took my mother and my best friend all in one sweep. I strug-gled with God being good, loving, caring, and compassionate. How could He be a God who honors family when He took my only real family here with me in the United States? I was left alone with a grief that felt too hard to escape. I even blamed my mother because I felt that she didn't fight to stay alive so that she could be with me.

During the extended period of time that the guilt lingered, I didn't remember my mother saying the day prior to her death how much she loved the place and that it was the best place she had lived. Instead, I blamed myself for buying the house and only later, realized the lie for what it was. I also recognized that my thoughts were being used against me for a purpose and on purpose. It's how the devil works: "When he lies, he speaks his native language, for he is a liar and the father of lies" (John 8:44, NIV). He is able to get us to forget what we know to be true and fills our heads and hearts with lies—all in an effort to further discourage and isolate us from God, and on me, it worked.

I keenly felt two of Kübler-Ross and Kessler's points: "Anger is strength, and it can be an anchor, giving temporary structure to the nothingness of loss. . . . [And] anger is just another indication of the intensity of your love."[72] I had to learn through my grief to be able to thank God for being given the opportunity to have a mother as great as my mother was and experiencing the blessings she brought to me and our family as it says to in James 1:17 (NIV) because "every good and perfect gift is from above, coming down from the Father of the heavenly lights."

The stage of bargaining was a unique and tricky one for me and not in the way the originators of the stages describe. I think what I did mainly was bargain about my own death because I didn't get a chance to bargain with God to save my mom's life. I asked several times why He didn't just kill me at the same time He took my mom. I also had moments of "What if. . . ?" but then those would automatically get me back to the anger stage. My "What if" statements" were mainly about me moving from Georgia to Ohio and buying that house. I got upset with myself because I believed that if I hadn't moved to Ohio and if I hadn't bought that house, my mother would still be alive.

In those moments, I forgot the promises of God applied to my mother as well, and it didn't matter where we lived or what house I bought. My mother's life was in God's hands. In Psalm 139:16 (NIV), King David stated, "All the days ordained for me were written in your book before one of them came to be." As a child of God herself, I forgot the truth of God's Word. They pertained to her in that moment of her death but also in her life. And, I had to believe, "Furthermore, because we are united with Christ, we have received an inheritance from God, for he chose us in advance, and he makes everything work out according to his plan" (Ephesians 1:11, NLT).

---

72 Elisabeth Kübler-Ross and David Kessler, *On Grief and Grieving.*

As far as the next stage, I have in previous sections gone through in detail the depression that seemed for me to be the prevailing stage that plagued me.

Acceptance was more gradual, and I realized that for me, acceptance had to come once I acknowledged the fact that God's will was done. I found solace in knowing that my mother and grandmother were with the Lord. I firmly believe that "to be absent from the body and to be present with the Lord" (2 Corinthians 5:8, NKJV). Acceptance meant that I had to receive God's will for my mom's life and my life, believing that He would continue to be with me and provide for me. I was not alone.

I would also have to say that acceptance and meaning traveled together. Kessler said, "But if we allow ourselves to move fully into this crucial and profound sixth stage—meaning—it will allow us to transform grief into something else, something rich and fulfilling."[73] I had to find meaning in my mom's death, and for me, that meant that I had to find a way to sustain the love I felt for her, still being able to move forward with my life in a positive way—one that honors her memory and honors God. Kessler states, and I wholeheartedly agree, "Those who are able to find meaning tend to have a much easier time grieving than those who don't."[74] So, at the time I was going through the sixth stage of grief, to be honest, I didn't know that there was a sixth stage to grief. Looking back, however, I can see where and how it applied at that season of my life.

Finding meaning in death first depends on our being able to find meaning in life. If I didn't believe that life had meaning, then

---

73 David Kessler, *Finding Meaning: The Sixth Stage of Grief.*
74 David Kessler, *Finding Meaning: The Sixth Stage of Grief.*

there is no way that I would have been able to find meaning in my mother's death. God had a plan for my life before I even came to be, and if I believed that for my life, I also had to believe that for the life of my mom and grandmother. We all know that death is unavoidable. In Hebrews 9:27 (KJV), we are told, "It is appointed unto men once to die," so as I accepted that God has a plan for our lives, it also meant that I had to accept that God had a plan in their deaths and how He chose to make them happen. So, as my healing came to fruition, I see it as the result of me finally grasping the reality of scripture and applying it to their deaths. My mother and my grandmother had fought the good fight and had finished their course. (See 2 Timothy 4:7.)

FINDING MEANING IN DEATH FIRST DEPENDS ON OUR BEING ABLE TO FIND MEANING IN LIFE.

THE FLESH IS WEAK, BUT THE SPIRIT IS WILLING

Even though we don't have foreknowledge, as Christians, we do know that God will always work things out for our good. So, we can walk in peace, and we can grab hold of the peace that surpasses all understanding so that it can guard our hearts and our minds in Christ Jesus during the detours of life that so often include the death of a loved one and other areas that lead to grief.

This passage has some of the most precious biblical promises and truths:

For you did not receive a spirit of slavery that returns you to fear, but you received the Spirit of sonship, by whom we cry, "Abba! Father!" The Spirit Himself testifies with our spirit that we are God's children. And if we are children, then we are heirs: heirs of God and co-heirs with Christ—if indeed we suffer with Him, so that we may also be glorified with Him. —Romans 8:15-17 (BSB)

It also is a sobering reminder that we will suffer in this life. We can be reassured that as joint heirs with Jesus, we, too, can cry out to our *Abba*, Father. We can know without a doubt, to quote Tye Tribbett's song, "We Gon' Be Alright,"[75] and that, like the scripture says, we may also be glorified with him.

We are told that the Holy Spirit helps in our weakness, and He intercedes for us in prayer according to the will of God. We also know and love the other verses that comfort, like Romans 8:31 (BSB): "If God is for us, who can be against us?" The chapter eloquently concludes by stating that nothing can separate us from God's love, plan, and purpose for our future. Several trials are listed, including afflictions, persecution, distress, famine, nakedness, danger, death, life, powers, anything created, things present, or things to come. Not one thing can break the bond that God the Father created between Himself and His children.

It's a great reminder that, through it all, if we just hold on to Jesus Christ—our rock, fortress, deliverer, shield, horn of our salvation, and stronghold—we will never walk alone. (See Psalm

---

75 Tye Tribbett, vocalist, "We Gon' Be Alright," by Tye Tribbett, released February 4, 2022, track 2 on *Kingdom Come*, UME—Global Clearing House.

18.) Jesus Christ, our Lord and Savior, died on the cross and then was raised from the dead. He is at the right hand of God, also interceding for us. God's love for me—for us—is rooted in Christ Jesus and was demonstrated by the shedding of His blood on Calvary's cross.

HE IS WITH YOU AS YOU WAIT FOR RELIEF

My medical issues didn't stop after my mom died. Instead, more scary things developed. In 2019, I underwent a kidney biopsy. It showed that lupus (SLE) was affecting my kidneys. I was diagnosed with lupus nephritis which required chemotherapy medications to prevent further damage to the kidney. Kidney failure is one of the biggest complications in patients with SLE because it can lead to the person needing dialysis. I was terrified that this would happen to me. At this time, I realized that there was another form of grief—loss of health—and I didn't want to face the need for dialysis or any worsening of the inflammation around my heart. I kept praying and asking for deliverance and healing, but it was not happening. In fact, it felt that I kept getting additional diagnoses.

Waiting on God can be difficult because it has the potential to lead to doubt, fear, and disbelief. In Isaiah 40:31, we are told that if we wait on the Lord, He will renew our strength. We will run and not be weary and walk and not faint. In that, I knew that I could, with God's help, make a change if I would just stop, be still, and listen to what He was wanting of me, waiting patiently to see what He would do next. God may choose to heal miraculously or do it via other means. I had been praying for direction for a long time and still do.

I pray for ears to hear from God and eyes to see what God wants to do and is already doing in my life. (See Matthew 13.) Our prayer should be that we never become like the Israelites that Isaiah spoke about in Isaiah 6. As we wait on His divine providence, let us not reject God's message or become spiritually deaf. Let us be eager to hear God and so attentive that we don't even miss Him if He comes as He did to Elijah in 1 Kings 19:11-12 in a still small voice or as He did to the prophet Samuel in 1 Samuel 3 in the night.

As I waited to hear from God, I knew I had to make changes to help my health, and one thing was to move from Portsmouth. I had several job opportunities that came up after my mother died. For a few, I sent my resume; for others, I interviewed. Some I just ignored. I was accepted to more than one but turned them down for various reasons. I felt that I wasn't ready to move, that leaving Portsmouth was deserting my mother who was buried there. Other times, I just felt that it wasn't the step God wanted me to take. I prayed often and fervently for direction. It eventually came in 2019 when I took the job in Cincinnati.

YOUR PAIN IS NO MATCH FOR GOD'S SOVEREIGNTY

Something that I hadn't realized is that God told Moses that Abraham, Isaac, and Jacob had known Him as God Almighty, "but I was not known to them by my name, 'the Lord'" (Exodus 6:3, CSB). I looked at that and thought, *Well, what's the difference? What exactly was God saying then, and what is He saying to me now?* First, I had to get the correct definition of "Lord" to truly grasp the significance of the verse.

The *King James Bible Dictionary* gives many definitions for Lord, depending on which word is used. *Jehovah* is God's proper name, but *Adon* means "one possessed of absolute control."[76] And it references *Webster's 1928 Dictionary* which gives the definition of Lord as "a master, a person possessing supreme power and authority; a ruler; a governor."[77] Upon reading this, it occurred to me that I can say that I love God and that I believe God, but the real question—or we might say the practical question—is the following: Is He truly *Lord* of my life? Is the Lord ruler of my life, my master, and the only person who has supreme power and authority over my life?

God knew that at that time in the book of Exodus, the Israelites didn't consider Him as Lord of their lives. I believe then for the Israelites as I believe now about my own life that God allowed certain things to happen so that they—and I—could see His signs, wonders, and majesty and ultimately grow closer to Him because I would realize my utter dependence on Him.

There are certain phrases or sentences in the Bible that will have us stop, pause, and go, "Wow." One of those occurs repeatedly in the story of the plagues in Exodus 7-11. God said, in Exodus 7:3 (NIV), "But I will harden Pharaoh's heart." What that meant is that instead of one plague, they had a total of ten, and the final involved the killing of the firstborn male. We may have to ask why, but we know that God had a divine, sovereign plan for why He allowed all of that to happen.

The best explanation I have for why this stuns me comes from Danish writer Søren Kierkegaard, regarded as the father of

---

76 "Lord," *King James Bible Dictionary*, https://www.kingjamesbibledictionary.com/Dictionary/lord.
77 "Lord," *Webster's Dictionary 1828*, https://webstersdictionary1828.com/Dictionary/Lord.

existentialism. His writing was felt to bring a specific discourse that would be used as a way of renewing Christian faith within Christendom during the time he lived. He made a famous statement: "Life can only be understood backwards; but it must be lived forward."[78] In twenty-first-century vernacular, we would probably say, "Hindsight is 20/20."

Can you see it now? This last plague led to the institution of the Passover, also called the Lord's Passover. In Exodus 12, God gave Moses instructions for getting an unblemished animal. It *had* to be perfect. That night, they were to take some of its blood and put it on the doorposts and the lintel of the houses where they ate some of the meat with unleavened bread and bitter herbs. This is just one of many references where we see that God pointed to His Son—our Savior, our Lord—who would be the unblemished first fruit, the Lamb of God whose blood had to be shed so that we could be raised to new life in Christ Jesus.

Living life in reverse, we can appreciate what was happening as we see how many more people—Jews and Gentiles, peoples of every tongue and tribe—would be saved for eternity because of THE PASSOVER LAMB, OUR LORD JESUS CHRIST.

God knew all that these things would happen, and He used the grief to move me forward to His goal and purpose for my life. He used the grief to highlight areas of my life that needed divine intervention—areas that I was trying to fix on my own but would never be able to. God is an amazing Father.

I woke up this morning with a migraine, so I decided to stay home from church and watch it online. I decided to also continue

---

78 Søren Kierkegaard, "Skrifter," *Journalen* JJ:167, vol. 18 (1843): 306. https://homepage.math.uiowa. edu/~jorgen/kierkegaardquotesource.html.

working on this chapter on grief. The Holy Spirit intervened and put a stamp on this book by what He said through Pastor Eric: "Sometimes it takes something painful to move us to the next stage," and in that same message, "God will never create a life in which He is not necessary." God will take our pain and work it into His ultimate plan for our lives. Pastor Eric also quoted several passages from my current Bible study, authored by Courtney Doctor, that I am doing on Romans.[79] It all just comes together because we can do all things through Christ who strengthens us and because Jesus and the Holy Spirit are both praying and interceding on our behalf.

GOD IS AN AMAZING FATHER.

As I look at God's mercies, I can only echo Paul in Romans 11:36 (BSB): "For from him and through him and to him are all things. To him be the glory forever. Amen."

---

79 Courtney Doctor, *In View of God's Mercies: The Gift of the Gospel in Romans* (Nashville, TN: LifeWay Press, 2022).

CHAPTER 7

Endurance Through the Race of Life

E nduring, by definition, is not easy. But we can take courage in the fact that Christ endured before us:

Therefore, since we also have such a large cloud of witnesses sur-rounding us, let us lay aside every hindrance and the sin that so easily ensnares us. Let us run with endurance the race that lies before us, keeping our eyes on Jesus, the source and perfecter of our faith. For the joy that lay before him, he endured the cross, despising the shame, and sat down at the right hand of the throne of God. —Hebrews 12:1–2 (CSB)

Interestingly, the Greek word for endurance is either *hupo-mone`* (feminine noun) or *hupomeno`* (verb). When used as a noun, *Strong's Concordance* says it means "a remaining behind, a patient enduring," and as a verb it means "to stay behind, to await and endure."[80] *Thayer's Greek Lexicon* speaks to enduring as stead-fastness and constancy when used in 1 Thessalonians 1:3 (NIV): "We remember before our God and Father your work produced by faith, your labor prompted by love, and your endurance inspired by hope in our Lord Jesus Christ," and James 5:11(CSB): "We count as blessed those who have endured." They are talking about the characteristics of a person who is unswerving in their delib-erate purpose and loyalty to faith and piety in even the greatest trials and sufferings.

It is helpful to note that enduring is both a noun and a verb. It is a state of being, but it is also something that we do. We must be the remnant—not those going with the crowd but those whom God has called for His plan and purpose and willing participants in the race. We function best when we have undergone the proper

---

80 Strong's Greek: 5281. Ὑπομονή (Hupomoné)—a Remaining behind, a Patient Enduring, https://biblehub.com/greek/5281.htm.

training, so in our race, we need endurance training (ET). Most of us have probably heard the term and related it to athletes preparing for an event. However, it is also used during rehabilitation after a stroke or heart attack. So, in the natural, there are several health benefits to endurance training: stronger muscles and increased blood flow and oxygen uptake that eventually lead to muscles working stronger and more efficiently.

As Christians, we must be able to withstand the fiery darts of the devil to be able to say we, too, are unswerving. So, what does our ET look like?

1) Accept the fact that you have to compete and that you have to train to succeed.

2) Acknowledge that you can't go the distance in haste. You'll need to mind your coach, emulate Jesus, and take the time. God is there waiting to welcome and assist; He hides us to find us.

3) Determine to keep digging. Don't give up until the race is over.

Some of us may feel intimidated by all the race analogies because, like me, you never played sports in school, and when possible, would try to do the very least you needed to make sure you passed physical education class. As a child going to school in Jamaica, I can remember that students were divided into "houses." Each year, the houses would compete against each other in athletics. Even if we were not one of the competitors, we all loved to cheer our team on to victory. I can remember being impressed by the contestants' athletic abilities and wishing I could do even half of what they were able to do. Of course, even with all that wishing, I wasn't *willing* to put in the work to achieve what they did.

In the United States, one of the highest-grossing television events is the Superbowl. In the rest of the world, it is probably the World Cup, and many love to watch the Olympic games. Most of us have never played, but we watch the games, host watch parties, or go to watch parties, all in the name of cheering on and hoping our team wins. We are in awe of the players' athletic prowess, their devotion to their craft, the hours they have to spend just to prepare, and the sheer brilliance of what they are able to push their bodies to do. Even if you are not one who likes to watch the Summer Olympics, most of us have heard of Usain Bolt. Usain Bolt, aka "Lightning Bolt," is a Jamaican sprinter considered one of the greatest athletes of all time.[81] He holds the record for the fastest man alive.[82] And he holds almost as many world titles and records as Michael Phelps.

YOU CAN'T GO THE DISTANCE IN HASTE

But, who holds the record for the fastest long-distance runner, a marathoner in races over 26.2 miles? His name is Eliud Kipchoge from Kenya, and he is considered the greatest male marathoner ever, since in Vienna in 2019, he ran a marathon in just under 2 hours.[83] Sports writer Matt Burgess wrote this article in 2019: "The incredible science behind Eliud Kipchoge's 1:59 marathon." In the article, the author makes reference to the fact that running a marathon in 1:59:59 would be equivalent to "running 100m

81 "Usain Bolt Biography, Olympic Medals, Records and Age," *Olympics.com*, https://olympics.com/en/athletes/usain-bolt.

82 Liam Gravvat, "Who Is the Fastest Person in the World? It's No Easy Answer, but Usain Bolt's Records Stand Tall," *USA Today*, 23 Sept. 2022, https://www.usatoday.com/story/sports/olympics/2022/09/23/who-fastest-person-world/10293358002/.

83 "Eliud Kipchoge Biography, Olympic Medals, Records and Age" *Olympics.com*, https://olympics.com/en/athletes/eliud-kipchoge.

sprints in just over 17 seconds—422 times in a row."[84] The ability to accomplish such a feat is absolutely amazing.

Paula Radcliffe from Great Britain ran the marathon, clocking the time at 2:15:25 in 2003. Hers remains the second fastest marathon ever run.[85] How is it that we are more aware of the sprinter than we are of the marathoners, even though their accomplishments are just as impressive and some may argue even more impressive? The world is obsessed with speed. Unfortunately, the race of life is not a sprint. We love to finish the race quickly, get our prize, sit down, be happy with the win, pat ourselves on our back, and be impressed about our accomplishment. However, life is more like a marathon, and there are no shortcuts. To get to the end, we must set a pace and keep moving forward.

In order to be successful in a marathon, the training is completely different compared to sprinting, even though they both involve running. As I thought about the race of life, I was intrigued by the history of marathons. How did the marathon become part of the Olympics? How long has it been a part of the Olympics? According to the *Encyclopedia Britannica*, the Battle of Marathon was fought in September 490 BCE as part of the Greco-Persian Wars. The battle was fought on the Marathon Plain of northeastern Attica where the Athenians "in a single afternoon, repulsed the first Persian invasion of Greece."[86]

Britannica says there is a known tale that became the basis for the modern marathon race. It is believed that an Athenian

---

84 Burgess, Matt "The Incredible Science behind Eliud Kipchoge's 1:59 Marathon," *WIRED UK*, 14 Oct. 2019, https://www.wired.co.uk/article/eliud-kipchoge-ineos-159-marathon.

85 "Paula Radcliffe Keeps Her Marathon World Record in IAAF about-Turn-" *The Guardian*, 10 Nov. 2011, https://www.theguardian.com/sport/2011/nov/10/paula-radcliffe-world-marathon-record.

86 "Battle of Marathon," *Encyclopædia Britannica*, 16 Mar. 2023, https://www.britannica.com/event/Battle-of-Marathon.

messenger was sent from Marathon to Athens, a distance of about twenty-five miles. After announcing the Persian defeat, he died from presumed exhaustion. It wasn't until the nineteenth century that the sport we now know as the marathon became part of the Olympics Games. According to the article titled "The Marathon: Its Long History & Where To Find The Best Events," the first modern Olympics was in Athens in 1896, and the first marathon race—only twenty-five miles—was part of this Olympics.[87]

However, as we know, in our modern day, the full marathon is 26.2 miles. It was in 1908 that the distance was increased, and it was finalized in 1921 as the official distance. The Olympics has several other sports that make up the entire Games, and different athletes often compete in different events. However, only in rare cases does one athlete participate in more than one sport. In our Christian life, we aren't all called to run the same race, but some of us may be called to run more than one race, or we may be facing several hardships.

Similar to the marathon, jumping hurdles was also part of the initial Olympic Games that began in 1896. One of the reasons that I absolutely love to watch this race is due to the fact that I am always in awe; not only are the people running fast, but as they are running, they have to navigate jumping over several obstacles set at fixed distances apart. According to Sportsmatik. com, there are numerous rules for this sport. Suppose the runner knocks down a hurdle while getting both legs over it. He or she is not disqualified. However, the runner has to stay in their lane. If the runner gets out of his or her lane, they are disqualified. If

---

87 Joshua Chiedu, "The Marathon: Its Long History & Where to Find the Best Events," *The Travel*, 7 Jan. 2022, https://www.thetravel.com/history-of-the-marathon-where-to-attend/.

the runner's hands knock over the hurdle or if the hurdle is intentionally knocked over, then the runner is disqualified.[88]

In track and field, another race is the relay. According to Olympics.com, the rules are many.[89] We typically see four runners on a team; however, the relay team can have six actual members. The rules allow for two additional athletes that can be substituted in later heats or in the final. Each runner has a portion that they must run before they pass the baton to the next runner. It goes like this until the race is completed. The baton is only passed within a designated "exchange zone," which is typically twenty meters long. If the baton is not passed in this zone, the team is disqualified. If the baton is dropped, the runner that was carrying the baton can leave his or her lane and retrieve it, but retrieving the baton cannot shorten the length of the race. The recipient of the baton can begin running before the change-over zone, and this allows the runner to achieve maximum acceleration and, in so doing, increases their potential of winning the race. Typically, when runners have finished their portion of the race, they stand on the side, cheering their team members on to victory.

Even though individual sports are different from team sports, there are several things that the athletes have in common. According to an article titled "How to Train Like an Olympian," the author states the following:

It's not just that most Olympians are born with a certain set of physiological gifts, although that's a big part of it. It's also their

---

88 "Hurdles Rules: How to Play, Basic Rules" *Sportsmatik*, 6 Aug. 2022, https://sportsmatik.com/sports-corner/sports-know-how/hurdles/rules.
89 "What Is a Relay Race? Know the Rules and the Records," *Olympics.com*, https://olympics.com/en/news/athletics-relay-races-rules-history-world-records-olympics.

commitment to their sports and, perhaps most important, the way they train.[90]

In the Bible, we are admonished frequently about running our own race but not what type of race we are running. In our spiritual race, we can use the analogies of sprinting, marathons, hurdles, and relays during different seasons, so the one race has all four types of events. I believe this one statement by Christ sums up so much about our spiritual race:

> *"If anyone desires to come after Me, let him deny himself, and take up his cross, and follow Me. For whoever desires to save his life will lose it, but whoever loses his life for My sake will find it!"* —*Matthew 16:24-25 (BLB)*

MIND YOUR COACH

As Christians, we are following Christ Jesus, conformed to the image of Christ, to be like him. We can think of our cross as the hurdles we jump and the baton we each must carry on our own. As we run the race in our own lanes, we come to realize that we are growing in faith and intimacy with God the Father, God the Son, and God the Holy Spirit. We run ultimately to lose our lives all so that we gain Christ. (See Philippians 3:8.)

In 2022, I did a Bible study on the book of Galatians, and in doing the study, my life was forever changed when I read Galatians 2:20 (NIV): "I have been crucified with Christ, and I no longer live, but Christ lives in me. The life I now live in the body, I live by faith in the Son of God, who loved me and gave himself for me."

---

90 "How to Train like an Olympian," *Forbes*, 8 July 2008, https://www.forbes.com/2008/07/08/training-perfect-athlete-olympics08-forbeslife-cx_avd_0708health.html?sh=2630bd4c79c1.

||||||||||||||||||||||||||||||||||||||||||||||||||||||||||||||||||||||||||||||||||||

AS WE RUN THE RACE IN OUR OWN LANES, WE COME TO REALIZE THAT WE ARE GROWING IN FAITH AND INTIMACY WITH GOD THE FATHER, GOD THE SON, AND GOD THE HOLY SPIRIT.

||||||||||||||||||||||||||||||||||||||||||||||||||||||||||||||||||||||||||||||||||||

A new and in-vogue concept is that of a life coach. One is the equivalent of what many of us who are older called mentors years ago. I have several friends who have life coaches and others who are in school to become life coaches. A life coach is used by many successful men and women who have the means to pay for the expertise to help them achieve their life goals. Athletes also have coaches. Coaches are there to teach, train, provide feedback, support growth, model, and facilitate best practices to achieve the desired outcomes.

In the Christian life, we also have a Life Coach, and He is personally given to every person who professes Jesus Christ as Lord and Savior and believes that He died for their sins. We have the indwelling Holy Spirit—the very Spirit of God Almighty. In John 16:7-8 (CSB), Jesus promised:

"Nevertheless, I am telling you the truth. It is for your benefit that I go away, because if I don't go away the Counselor will not come to you. If I go, I will send him to you. When he comes, he will convict the world about sin, righteousness, and judgment."

Jesus made further statements about our Life Coach who is free to us but bought with the blood of Jesus on the cross at Calvary:

"When the Spirit of truth comes, he will guide you into all the truth. For he will not speak on his own, but he will speak whatever he hears. He will also declare to you what is to come. He will glorify me, because he will take from what is mine and declare it to you. Everything the Father has is mine. This is why I told you that he takes from what is mine and will declare it to you."
—*John 16:13-15 (CSB)*

It is imperative that we listen to the Holy Spirit and live a life that allows His voice to be easily heard among the noise of the world. The Holy Spirit cannot speak to us if we, in running the race, are not being obedient because it then becomes harder and harder to hear His voice and to follow His guidance. We may choose other coaches, and in so doing, it may cost us more than money. It can cost us time, our lives, or the lives of others.

As I thought about the final chapter of this book, I immediately thought about the cloud of witnesses in Hebrews 12. I believe my mother, grandmother, and the great men and women of the Bible are in the cloud of witnesses. Second, in any race, we need someone to cheer us on to victory. Paul's description of the great cloud of witnesses is not to say that they are in heaven, constantly looking down on us and clapping. Instead, the great cloud of witnesses serves as encouragers based on what we have read about them in the Bible and what they had to endure. They were our loved ones. We are aware of what they had to endure to become a "witness," and we can be encouraged as we each run our own race and scale our own hurdles. We can see how their faith in God allowed them to persevere and how God moved on their behalf.

LOOK LIKE JESUS, WALK LIKE JESUS, TALK LIKE JESUS

We must endure to the end, not just to get the victory. When we all get to the end, victory is already ours, and if we remain steadfast, we will not just get a gold medal—but a crown: "Blessed is the man who remains steadfast under trial, for when he has stood the test he will receive the crown of life, which God has promised to those who love him" (James 1:12, ESV). James 5:11 (CSB) says, "See, we count as blessed those who have endured. You have heard of Job's endurance and have seen the outcome that the Lord brought about. The Lord is compassionate and merciful."

We know that there are several distinctions between our spiritual race and Olympic races. Athletes in the natural race for victory and glory, but like my worship leader Pastor Blake Mason from Citygate Church likes to say, "We fight not for victory but from Victory." We already have the victory because of Jesus (See 1 Corinthians 15:57.) and the power of the cross (See 1 Corinthians 1:18.). Also, we are told throughout the Scriptures to honor God in all we do. We do what we do not so that we become famous and we get the glory, but we do it so that God gets the glory: "So, whether you eat or drink, or whatever you do, do everything for the glory of God" (1 Corinthians 10:31, CSB).

Most great athletes have someone—that one person that they look up to, they have always admired, and they've always wanted to be like. That person is our Savior and Lord Jesus Christ, the author and perfector of our faith. We are told in Romans 13:14 (ESV), "But put on the Lord Jesus Christ." We know that in putting on the Lord Jesus, it means that we ought to be imitating Jesus to the point that if someone were to see us or hear us, they would think that we are Jesus because our actions so resemble Him.

Jesus Christ tells us that we ought to imitate him:

» "For I have given you an example, that you also should do just as I have done for you." (John 13:15, CSB)

» "Whoever serves me must follow me." (John 12:26, NIV)

» "Learn of me; for I am meek and humble of heart." (Matthew 11:29, KJV)

» "I have glorified You on the earth. I have finished the work which You have given Me to do." (John 17:4, NKJV)

Our perfect example, Christ Jesus, also showed us what we ought to do when the cross we are called to bear seems overwhelming—when we know without a doubt that what we are going through is part of God's purpose and plan for our lives. In the garden at Gethsemane, we see Jesus praying. He already knew what was coming and was committed to going to the cross. However, we hear him praying, "Father, if it is Your will, take this cup away from Me; nevertheless not My will, but Yours, be done" (Luke 22:42, NKJV). Jesus exemplified perfect obedience, but what really resonates with me is that He was honest with God. Our Father God did not chastise Him for His honesty in saying what we sometimes want to say when we are going through our own race, and we are met with a hurdle that we don't want to deal with. Instead, God sent an angel from heaven to strengthen him. So, be honest with God.

We might say things like, "God, I am afraid," "God, I don't have the words or the talent to do this," "Father, I am not qualified for this," or "God, why me?" We might say, "I really think you should ask someone else, God," or "I do not have what it takes to do this." Or we may simply be disobedient and say no, pull away, or ignore Him because we don't want to do what He has asked us to do. Instead of listening, we might go off on a different path. The devil might start to tell us why we should not listen to God or why we shouldn't trust God. He might encourage us to "Do you," "Live your truth," "God doesn't want you to be happy," "You have to do what you think makes you happy," or "You are the only one responsible for your future," and before we know it, we are making the wrong decisions, and we might end up with consequences that are hard to live with.

We might end up so far down a path that we have forgotten the original path. Instead of being a help to others, we end up helping others down the wrong path and far from the original plan and purpose for which they were created. However, once we come to the realization that we have sinned, and we have made the wrong choice in straying from God, He can and will use even the bad decisions in our lives to accomplish what He created us to do.

Sometimes God may work in such a way that He rescues us from going through things. He may create a path for us to avoid certain hurdles. We are running late and end up not being in that accident, or like my suicide attempt, I had the plan and the means but was saved from the event. Sometimes, He allows us to be rescued out of things, and when that happens, we like the Hebrew boys, come out of the fire not smelling like smoke. Joseph went through several trials after he was sold into slavery, but each time God pulled him out of one thing, he was promoted to another until, ultimately, he was able to say that what his brothers had planned for evil, God used for good and to save many lives. And like Joseph, many times, our purpose is tied to someone else's story. Living out our God-given purpose will affect our life, but it affects others as well. Others may be waiting on us to accept our call, to take our baton, and to run our race so that they can live in the purpose God created for them.

TAKE THE TIME TO TRAIN

God can allow things to happen and allow those things to change us. I often think of myself, with multiple health diagnoses, scares, and intense grief and how those things were used, over time, to build my faith, drawing me closer to God, strengthening my dependence on Him, and teaching me about full daily surrender, sacrifice, and true worship. Enduring our hardships as we run means that we must have faith, trust God to mean what He says, and believe that all His promises are "Yes" and "Amen." (See 2 Corinthians 1:20.)

GOD CAN ALLOW THINGS TO HAPPEN AND ALLOW THOSE THINGS TO CHANGE US.

A key aspect of being a successful Olympian is taking the time to train before the competition. While we don't "compete" as Olympians do, we are in a race with the enemy of our souls, so we have to spend the requisite amount of time in training, making sacrifices in the now that will be beneficial so that we can cross the finish line as victors. We have to make sure we train for our race so that we can be prepared for each hurdle that we will meet along the race of life. We have to be ready to run well when we embark upon each trial. Training involves first believing in Jesus Christ. We must also be members of a Bible-believing church, spend time in personal prayer, read our Bibles, study on our own, and spend time in public and private worship.

The story that unfolds as Moses and his brother, Aaron, went to Pharaoh and asked that he release the Israelites is well known because it did not happen immediately. God hardened the heart of Pharaoh and by doing this, delayed the release of God's chosen people. It truly is a powerful story of endurance, faith, and trust in the one true God. The Divine Author placed this story in the Bible as an example for us.

At times, when the road gets harder and we get more detours and more delays, it isn't always from the enemy. We see that in delaying His promise to His people, God was ensuring that the enemy would see that God only is the *Great I AM*. In every detour, we can pause and look to see where God is at work. As the delays continued, they also allowed the Israelites to endure so that they could be allowed to see different characteristics of God. As we wait through different hardships and undergo endurance training, the names of God become personal. He becomes all of these to us:

- » Abba Father
- » Adonai (the Lord)
- » Alpha and Omega (the Beginning and End)
- » Christos (the Anointed One)
- » El Deah (the God of Knowledge)
- » El Elyon (the God Most High)

- » El Olam (the Everlasting God)
- » El Roi (the God Who Sees)
- » Elohim (the Creator)
- » Yahweh (I AM)
- » El Shaddai (God Almighty)
- » Jehovah-Jireh (the Lord Will Provide)
- » Jehovah-Nissi (the Lord my Banner)
- » Jehovah-Rapha (the Lord that Heals)
- » Jehovah-Sabbaoth (the Lord of Hosts)
- » Jehovah-Shalom (the Lord is Peace)
- » Jehovah-Shammah (the Lord is There)
- » Jehovah Tsidkenu (the Lord our Righteousness)[91]

We get to not only know of God, but we get to have a more intimate relationship with Him, and we get to know God. The relationship will only get stronger with time as our trust grows deeper in Him, and eventually, God Himself can trust us.

We read about Job in chapter 4. Job was a man of integrity. He feared God and shunned evil. He was blessed with his ten children, estates, and animals. He was the most noble man in his area of the world. And, at the devil's hand, Job lost everything. The devil may try to harm us in all kinds of ways, but he knows he has God-imposed limitations, and unless the Lord allows it, there's only so much he can do. As scary as this is, it is also comforting because we see that God always has us in His sight and His hands. If He allows certain trials, they will work for our good, and He will get the glory from our obedience.

---

91 "The Names of God Found in the Bible," *Love Worth Finding Ministries*, https://www.lwf.org/names-of-god?gad=1&gclid=CjwKCAjw9J2iBhBPEiwAErwpeYmgYTlaXsxs2XqL3ctVzNK-Ct_IYczrLc9Q5OeYyBMgaXsxQwll8hoCkQEQAvD_BwE.

How we endure is important. Do we curse God, or do we continue to give God glory, be thankful, and worship despite hardship? The devil isn't going to be happy until he gets us to curse God.

GOD WELCOMES YOU AS YOU WRESTLE

In Job's case, Satan had to ask for permission, but still, there was built-in protection, and he had limits. The devil cannot tell the future, and he didn't realize that asking for what he did ultimately led to Job being even more blessed. Satan may have felt he was the one doing the destruction, but God said that Satan had incited Him—God—to destroy Job. (See Job 2:3.) The statement may be hard to swallow, but it also tells us that Satan doesn't have as much power as we assign to him. Nothing comes to us that first doesn't pass through God's fingers. If it passes through His fingers, we are meant to learn from it. It is being used to refine us.

It can also be used as a testimony for others. One of Job's friends, Eliphaz, had just finished his discourse, telling Job what he thought about his hardship. Basically, Eliphaz thought Job's hardships were just. In Job 23, Job defended himself, candidly speaking and conveying what some of us would probably say or want to say to God as we are scaling one hurdle after the other, dropping the baton, or missing the transfer. What was Job's response?

Job replied:

"I'm not letting up—I'm standing my ground.
My complaint is legitimate.
God has no right to treat me like this—
it isn't fair!
If I knew where on earth to find him,

I'd go straight to him.
I'd lay my case before him face-to-face,
 give him all my arguments firsthand.
I'd find out exactly what he's thinking,
 discover what's going on in his head.
Do you think he'd dismiss me or bully me?
No, he'd take me seriously.
He'd see a straight-living man standing before him;
 my Judge would acquit me for good of all charges."
—Job 23:1-7 (MSG)

Isn't this what we would want to say as the race gets too arduous? So often, we are told not to question God, but we can, and Job shows us that we can. King David, throughout the book of Psalms, shows us we can too. When we feel like giving up, we may question God, but ultimately, we can trust Him. Hardships may be tests, but we can do one test at a time, one race at a time, or one hurdle at a time. I pray that you and I will be able to say: "Yet he knows the way I have taken; when he has tested me, I will emerge as pure gold" (Job 23:10, CSB).

We briefly touched on Jacob in chapter 2. In Genesis 32, there is a well-known story of Jacob wrestling with a man. Jacob was on his way back home with his family and all his possessions, but he feared his brother Esau, from whom he had stolen the birthright. He divided his entourage in two, one with gifts for his brother, which he sent on ahead, and the second including his two wives, female servants, and eleven sons. He had them stay behind.

Then Jacob decided to spend the night alone and had a fascinating dream:

A man wrestled with him till daybreak. When the man saw that he could not overpower him, he touched the socket of Jacob's hip so that his hip was wrenched as he wrestled with the man. Then the man said, "Let me go, for it is daybreak."

But Jacob replied, "I will not let you go unless you bless me."

The man asked him, "What is your name?"

"Jacob," he answered.

Then the man said, "Your name will no longer be Jacob, but Israel, because you have struggled with God and with humans and have overcome."

Jacob said, "Please tell me your name."

But he replied, "Why do you ask my name?" Then he blessed him there.

So Jacob called the place Peniel, saying, "It is because I saw God face to face, and yet my life was spared." —Genesis 32:24-30 (NIV)

"Jacob" means supplanter or usurper, which is not a great moniker to be known by. It implies that the person bearing that name is not to be trusted because they can be deceitful. However, when Jacob wrestled with God and was winning, he didn't let go because he wanted a blessing. At some point, Jacob realized he had been wrestling with God.

The point I'm trying to make is that sometimes when we are first facing a hardship, we may not realize that we are wrestling with God—our endurance is against the Lord—but when we do, the rules change. The expected outcome also changes. We don't want to just finish; we don't just want to win. Now we want a blessing! Jacob did not want more wealth, wives, children, or health; instead, what he got was a *name change*. In the Old

Testament, more so than today, great emphasis was placed on someone's name. I read an article written by Chana Weisberg titled "Can a Change of Name Create a Change of Destiny?" She states that it is believed that a child's destiny is wrapped up in the combination of Hebrew letters that make up his or her name.[92]

So, the importance here is that even though Jacob didn't choose his name, he lived up to the meaning of his name when he cheated his twin brother out of his birthright. The deceit started in the womb. Seven chapters earlier in Genesis 25, we are told how Isaac prayed for his wife, Rebekah, because she was childless. During her pregnancy, the babies were fighting in her womb. She inquired of the Lord and was told:

> *"Two nations are in your womb; two peoples will come from you and be separated; one people will be stronger than the other, and the older will serve the younger. . . . The first one came out red-looking, covered with hair like a fur coat, and they named him Esau. After this, his brother came out grasping Esau's heel with his hand. So he was named Jacob."* —Genesis 25:23 and 25 (CSB)

Names and labels carry such power that many of us consciously or unconsciously start to change our behavior to match our names. As we start to incorporate those behaviors into our identity, we become a version of ourselves that we don't like but feel powerless to change. In essence, what is happening is dependent on neuroplasticity. Neuroplasticity is the brain's ability to change and adapt both structurally and functionally. These changes occur throughout life and are dependent on life experiences.

---

92 Chana Weisberg, "Can a Change of Name Create a Change of Destiny?" *The Jewish Woman*, https://www.chabad.org/theJewishWoman/article_cdo/aid/2235035/jewish/Can-a-Change-of-Name-Create-a-Change-of-Destiny.htm.

Susannah Cahalan, author of *Brain on Fire: My Month of Madness,* was invited to an American Academy of Neurology conference I attended to talk about her journey with anti-NMDA encephalitis. In her book, she said, "Our minds have the incredible capacity to both alter the strength of connections among neurons, essentially rewiring them, and create entirely new pathways."[93] So, we begin to believe what we have been told about our names, and we let them shape who we become as we allow new neuronal pathways to be formed.

We can now realize how much of a blessing the name change was. He went from Jacob the usurper to Israel: the one who struggles with God, one who is triumphant with God, who contends with God.[94] So, even though he didn't get material things as a blessing with the name change, he got so much more. He got a new identity, one associated with strength and power!

Contending, biblically speaking, is fighting for something until we see it happen or until everything is set up for it spiritually. During hardships sometimes, we must contend with God for ourselves and for other people as well. As we continue our endurance training, we realize that we are also fighting to be blessed. It doesn't make sense what is happening, but I encourage you to keep holding onto God. We should keep pleading and not let go until we get our blessing, until we are triumphant. We can go from being called a sinner to a sinner saved by grace, from an addict to more than a conqueror, from anxiety to peace, from living with depression to the joy of the Lord, from having a diagnosis

93 Susannah Cahalan, *Brain on Fire: My Month of Madness* (New York, NY: Simon & Schuster, 2022).
94 "Israel" *SheKnows,* 22 Aug. 2018, https://www.sheknows.com/baby-names/name/israel/.

of cancer to being a survivor, from surviving to thriving in every aspect of our lives, and the list goes on and on.

Like Jacob, let's come out of our wrestling with God changed with a new name and a new identity in Christ; instead of being labeled with sickness, negativity, and death, we can put on new birth in Jesus Christ. We may come out of the wrestling match with scars. Some may be visible, like Israel, who limped after his face-to-face encounter with God, but not all of them, and others will know that we have been with the Lord. Scars tell a story; they may not look pretty, but they attest that we were able to hold on long enough to become an overcomer.

HE HIDES YOU TO FIND YOU, SO HOLD ON A LITTLE LONGER

In 1 Kings 17, we read about the prophet Elijah. His path in this one chapter was quite circuitous. He came on the scene in the presence of King Ahab. How he got there, we don't know, but because of being obedient to God, he became enemy number one of King Ahab and Queen Jezebel. After telling the king what God intended to do because of Israel's idolatry, God immediately pulled Elijah away and told him to go and hide. God sent him to the Wadi (Brook) Cherith and commanded ravens to feed him.

One minute, Elijah was in the presence of a king, thinking that big things were going to happen. Then, he was told to hide. This was probably not the path he thought his race would take him on. The word *Cherith* meant isolation, and it represented for Elijah and for us a place where God hides and isolates us usually because He is preparing us for something bigger. Colin

Smith, in his article "Has God given You a Cherith Experience?" states the following:

> Cherith is the place where God hides you and holds back what you most want to do. Don't count it a strange thing if God hides you. Here's the principle: When God chooses to hide you for a time, He is preparing you for a greater purpose.[95]

Some of us can probably relate to this in some way. I know I can. I finally got a job that was paying me an adequate amount of money, bought a house, and moved to Portsmouth. Then a freak accident killed my mother. I was left alone in a new environment with no family nearby, and my closest family was living in Jamaica, West Indies. Isolation.

God, however, provided for Elijah at a brook during a drought and allowed ravens to feed him. Ravens belong to a species of the genus *Corvus*. According to *Encyclopedia Britannica*, the common raven historically was a universal symbol of dark prophecy— of death, pestilence and disease.[96] Some ravens are considered notorious nest-robbers and also have gained notoriety for being unpopular with farmers because they will raid crops and can be destructive. They like to store their food for later consumption. They will steal from other animals and also can be a nuisance to humans as well, flying off with mail, pulling clothespins off lines, and even taking car keys.

So, here we see God putting Elijah in isolation but tending to him and using an unlikely thing to provide food. A bird that would prefer to steal and store away for itself was used by God to provide food for a human. Never doubt whom God can use

---

95 Colin Smith, "Has God given You a Cherith Experience?" *Open the Bible*, 13 Dec. 2018, https://openthebible.org/article/has-god-given-you-a-cherith-experience/.

96 "Raven" *Encyclopædia Britannica*, https://www.britannica.com/animal/raven.

to accomplish His plan and purpose if they remain obedient to the directions of their Coach. At times during our isolation, we don't always understand or see the blessing until after the period of isolation is over.

||||||||||||||||||||||||||||||||||||||||||||||||||||||||||||||||||||||||||||||||||||||||||||||||||||||||

NEVER DOUBT WHOM GOD CAN USE TO ACCOMPLISH HIS PLAN AND PURPOSE IF THEY REMAIN OBEDIENT TO THE DIRECTIONS OF THEIR COACH.

||||||||||||||||||||||||||||||||||||||||||||||||||||||||||||||||||||||||||||||||||||||||||||||||||||||||

After he had raised a widow's son, we are told that Elijah went to seek out King Ahab. He first met up with Obadiah. Then, in 1 Kings 18:10 (CSB), Obadiah said, "As the Lord your God lives, there is no nation or kingdom where my lord [King Ahab] has not sent someone to search for you." During the period of time that Elijah was alone at the Brook Cherith, when he was with the widow at Zarephath, and when he was away from family and loved ones, he was being protected because if Ahab had found him, he probably would have had him killed.

In our endurance training, during our periods of hardship, of wrestling, we may feel isolated and abandoned by God Himself. However, like Elijah, we can keep on course, doing what He has called us to do, even if it doesn't make sense or line up with what we know to be our destiny. Our obedience will pay off.

King David, prior to coming to the kingdom, was out in the field tending sheep. He was, in essence, in isolation also because he was anointed as king but kept in a field instead of going to the palace. However, in 1 Samuel 17, we are told that it was in the field that he learned how to kill a bear and lion with his bare hands. He was by himself in his isolation but doing what he was already called to do until God's appointed time for him to move to the next stage of his life on the road to his destiny.

In his obedience, we see that his confidence in God and his strength were built up so that he was able to come unafraid to defeat Goliath, the uncircumcised Philistine. He was able to boldly say in verse 37 (CSB), "The Lord who saved me from the paw of the lion and the paw of the bear will save me from the hand of this Philistine." If David hadn't had the experiences in the field, he would have been like all the other men of Israel—including the current king—afraid of Goliath.

So, as we trust God, His timing, and His plan, we will see in our own lives that periods of isolation can be periods of protection, but they can also be periods of growth. God can and will use those periods to bring to light hidden strengths. Those things that He can uncover within us will help us to be better equipped to handle the blessing, the promotion, and the next stage that He is preparing us for. However, these periods can also unmask areas in our lives that need to be burned on the altar so that we can truly become living sacrifices, equipped and ready to be used by God for His plan and purpose.

The next instruction Elijah was given came after God allowed His provision to stop; God had another destination in place. In 1 Kings17:8 (CSB), God told Elijah, "Get up, go to Zarephath that belongs to Sidon and stay there. Look, I have commanded a woman who is a widow to provide for you there."

Isn't this just like God? We are running along, and we think we have just scaled a hurdle and figure we will be given a reprieve for a while. We hope it will last for years, but then, right away, the Holy Spirit lets us know that it is time to move. God didn't give Elijah all the information, and that happens in our lives too. We are first tested on our obedience before we can figure out what we are to learn from the experience.

Sidon was where Queen Jezebel came from. It was a region that was known for worshiping Baal. In fact, the king of the Phoenicians who was Queen Jezebel's father, was called Ethbaal of Tyre. So, God was sending His prophet to a non-Israelite region—a region full of people who didn't believe in God but worshiped Baal. God was using a Baal worshiper to provide for Elijah. I am sure Elijah knew that the region was filled with idolatry, but he was obedient, and he went. His time in isolation at the Brook Cherith probably taught him that when God spoke, even if he didn't feel like doing it, he had to be obedient.

Zarephath means a place of refinement, smelter, smelting place, place of purification, place of purity, and a place of trial. Can you believe this? I know it was hard to see it and believe it, but yes, throughout life, we will see that as we unpack our bags for the race, and as we run the race, God will ask us to do things or go to places that we would rather not. However, could it be that some of the trials and tribulations are our Zarephath—a place that God will use for our refinement, for our purification, if we just remain faithful and allow Him to do His work through the process?

God told Elijah that He had provided a widow to provide for him, but He didn't tell him that two miracles would happen as a result of his obedience that would highly benefit this widow and her son. So, our obedience is not just for us but for God's glory, and we should always be mindful that others are probably waiting on us to walk in our purpose so that they can see the hand of God in their lives. First Kings 17:16 (CSB) describes how "the [widow's] flour jar did not become empty, and the oil jug did not run dry, according to the word of the Lord he had spoken through Elijah." And later in verse 22 (CSB), after the widow's son had died, "the Lord listened to Elijah, and the boy's life came into him again, and he lived." And the widow—a Baal worshiper—in verse 24 (CSB) said, "Now I know you are a man of God and the Lord's word from your mouth is true."

IF YOU WANT TO FIND THE GOLD, YOU HAVE TO KEEP DIGGING

Our redemption has always been part of God's plan. If it weren't for Jesus, we would be eternally lost. Everything in our lives was orchestrated from the very beginning. Even before we came to be, God had a purpose, and we were created for that purpose.

The institution of the Passover arose out of the Israelites' slavery and just prior to their deliverance from captivity. The Israelites already had been going over one hurdle after the next and were now being given a new ritual with many uncertainties. We, however, are blessed just because we have read the book and believed!

John 17:1-4 (HCSB) is just one of many references in the Old Testament where we see God pointing to His Hon, our unblemished Passover Lamb, our Redeemer who would die on a cross for our sins as part of His race that he decided to run the race the Father had chosen for him:

> *Jesus spoke these things, looked up to heaven, and said: "Father, the hour has come. Glorify your Son so that the Son may glorify you, since you gave him authority over all flesh, so that he may give eternal life to everyone you have given him. This is eternal life; that they may know you, the only true God, and the one you have sent—Jesus Christ. I have glorified you on the earth by completing the work you gave me to do."*

Our Savior and Lord, Jesus, would be the unblemished lamb, the first fruits, the Lamb of God whose blood had to be shed so that we could be raised to new life and guaranteed eternity with God the Father. I am covered by the blood, washed in the blood, and delivered by the blood. And, I share in Christ's sufferings as a result:

> *To this you were called, because Christ suffered for you, leaving you an example, that you should follow in his steps. When they hurled their insults at him, he did not retaliate, when he suffered, he made no threats. Instead, he entrusted himself to him who judges justly. —1 Peter 2:21-23 (CSB)*

So, by living life in reverse, realizing that God never does anything without a purpose, we can appreciate what has happened in the past, what is happening right now, and what is going to happen in the future. We serve the God of the Impossible, who leads us down the path to redemption through numerous detours. He gives and takes away and guides us through the wilderness—all while training us to overcome hardships and develop endurance because nothing is wasted.

My goal is to be able to say, like the apostle Paul:

Not that I have already reached the goal or am already perfect, but I make every effort to take hold of it because I also have been taken hold of by Christ Jesus. Brothers and sisters, I do not consider myself to have taken hold of it. But one thing I do: Forgetting what is behind and reaching forward to what is ahead, I pursue as my goal the prize promised by God's heavenly call in Christ Jesus. —Philippians 3:12-13 (CSB)

Printed in the USA
CPSIA information can be obtained
at www.ICGtesting.com
LVHW011406280723
753395LV00016B/1024